THE MBE REVOLUTION
MISSION-BASED ENTREPRENEUR

DEVELOPING ECONOMIC ENGINES THAT
DRIVE MISSION-BASED MOVEMENTS

BY ERIC BAHME
FOREWORD BY HORST SCHULZE
FOUNDING PRESIDENT AND FORMER COO
OF THE RITZ-CARLTON HOTEL COMPANY

KingdomPoint
international

Eric Bahme
The MBE Revolution: Developing Economic Engines that Drive Mission-based Movements

© 2009 Eric Bahme

9727 NE Sandy Boulevard
Portland, Oregon 97220
800-820-9759
503-296-2459 FAX

eric@KingdomPoint.com

www.KingdomPoint.com

The following abbreviations are used to identify versions of the Bible used in this book:

NIV Scripture taken from the HOLY BIBLE, NEW INTERNATIONAL VERSION®. Copyright © 1973, 1978, 1984 International Bible Society. Used by permission of Zondervan. All rights reserved. The "NIV" and "New International Version" trademarks are registered in the United States Patent and Trademark Office by International Bible Society. Use of either trademark requires the permission of International Bible Society.

KJV *King James Version,* also known as the *Authorized Version.*

NKJV *New King James Version.* Copyright © 1982 by Thomas Nelson, Inc.
Used by permission. All rights reserved.

The Message The Message, The Bible in Contemporary Language, by Eugene H. Peterson. Scripture taken from *The Message* Copyright © 1993, 1994, 1995, 1996, 2000, 2001, 2002.
Used by permission of NavPress Publishing Group.

NLT Scripture quotations marked NLT are taken from the Holy Bible, *New Living Translation,* copyright 1996, 2004. Used by permission of Tyndale House Publishers, Inc., Wheaton, Illinois 60189.
All rights reserved.

Includes bibliographical references.

ISBN 978-0-9842177-1-7 (trade paper)

© 2009 Eric Bahme

Publishing and marketing support provided by Jeff Pederson at JPED Publsihing Group—jpedpublishing.com

DEDICATIONS

This book is dedicated to my family.

My wife Rita and daughter Alyssa—Without you there wouldn't be a story to tell. Together you have written these chapters in my soul.

My sister-in-law and brother-in-law, Judy and Jeff—You have followed and served so faithfully. You are the definition of loyalty and love.

My nephews Brian and Kristofer—Rock on, young entrepreneurs. An uncle could never be more proud.

Eastside Church—You are the greatest people of servant leaders a pastor could ever ask for. You have fostered this vision to even greater heights.

WHAT CAN I DO TO MAKE A DIFFERENCE?

For the most part, everyone wants to make a difference in the world. The overwhelming question is how? It is easy to grow indifferent, unresponsive and numb to the world's plight. What can one person really do to change the world? At the same time, so many of us long to be part of something bigger than ourselves—a transformation of revolutionary proportions. Yet it is easy to become pessimistic in our outlook if we're not careful.

You hold in your hands a book that can make a difference in so many lives and as you read the pages you might be tempted to say "this really doesn't apply to me, I'm not a leader who can build a hotel or start a business." While you might not be in a place to implement the story of this book, you can help ignite the fires of this revolution.

Today, the role of the church and many nonprofits has been so narrowly defined and lived out that many of these organizations have lost touch with the communities they are supposed to serve. Two reasons are often the culprit: First, congregations and groups no longer know how to engage with people who are different than themselves. Second, funding new endeavors and fresh vision is becoming increasingly difficult as donor fatigue produces rigor mortis within the organization.

If we could infuse our organizations with the ability to reengage their communities and at the same time become fully sustainable we could create an innovative revolution of significant proportion. This book will show a leader how to do this. If you change the leader, you change the organization. I believe that everything rises and falls with leadership. Good leadership can produce great change. Stagnant leadership will produce death.

KingdomPoint is committed to getting a copy of this book into the hands of every Christian leader in our nation and around the world. We believe that the message of this book can spark dreams, vision, hope and engagement with pre-Christian people and at the same time create an economic engine for community transformation.

Would you become a partner in this revolution? Help us get a copy of this book into the hands of every Christian thought leader in our nation and around the world. Go to www.KingdomPoint.com and purchase multiple copies of this book. The books you buy will be distributed to leaders who can make a difference. You will receive the names and communities where each book was sent, knowing that you have helped spawn a revolution.

Your investment in this book is an investment in a leader. It could reproduce this story in communities all across the world, helping the church move back out into the streets and creating a way to sustain ministry for years to come. Imagine a leader who reads this book because of your partnership and then leads his church to connect with the community through business, having thousands of people discover a relationship with Christ and giving the ministry hundreds of thousands of new dollars each year to do ministry that once was never possible. Now imagine this multiplied over and over again—organizations joining forces together, combining resources, giving away, sharing the message and aggressively advancing the Kingdom. This, my friend, is an MBE Revolution.

ORDER YOUR COPIES FOR MINISTRIES TODAY AT
www.KingdomPoint.com

CONTENTS

DOES YOUR CHURCH OWN ALL THIS?

One question comes up nearly every day on our hotel campus at the Portland Airport Quality Inn and Suites and the Rodeway Inn.

"Does your church own all this?"

Our simple answer is "Yes."

Since our church bought these neighboring hotels in Portland, OR, we have touched the lives of tens of thousands of people. We have a new "congregation" every night, including hotel guests, coffee shop customers and neighbors with practical needs who watch us live out the Gospel through acts of hospitable service.

Through our church (that owns the hotel and meets in the hotel conference center), we are transforming our community and seeing the lives of people changed.

Through our hotel business model, we have helped fund a recovery center, a homeless shelter, a job-training program and many other ministries.

This book is a story of hopes and dreams come true. It is a journey of faith and a discovery of identity. It opens the door to a world of true prosperity that the Church has almost forgotten still exists.

This book is an invitation for you to follow the same path.

—Eric Bahme
Portland, OR, 2009

FOREWORD

BY HORST SCHULZE

Every human being has a soul and a purpose. We have been created to make a difference in the world. At work, every employee should understand that he has a purpose and is vital to the organization. When I first met Pastor Eric Bahme he expressed to me that same fundamental thinking and I was happy to talk with him and support and mentor him. I am convinced that the world needs more leaders today and I want to help raise them up.

When I was just 11 years old, I announced that I wanted to work in a hotel. Never mind that I had never even set foot in one. I had a dream and I wanted to follow it. You will read in this book that following your dreams is important. In fact, it is critical. Everyone can have a dream, from the dishwasher to the front desk clerk in a hotel. It is important to never give up on your dreams.

Three years after I made that announcement, I quit school and went off to be a busboy at a hotel 110 miles from home. My mother warned me to behave, I remember, because the hotel was fancy and the guests were "important people." When I met the maître d' of the restaurant, I knew what my mother meant. The maître d' was exceptional in his position. When he entered the room, you felt his presence. People felt honored when he came to their table. He achieved respect because he created excellence in all that he did. He was as important to the guests as they were to him.

That image of excellence has dominated my thinking and from that time on, I have spent my whole life serving people, being involved in their lives and creating places of excellence for their benefit. In any organization, developing excellent employees with a service mindset takes hard work and attention to details. Some view service as menial, but it was clear to me early on that service is an art. It is also a privilege and it is from this vantage point that Pastor Eric has written this book.

In my opinion, most companies are hiring employees, as a rule, to perform certain functions. They hire housekeepers to clean rooms, dishwashers to wash dishes, front desk agents to work the desk. However, people should be hired to fulfill the objectives and values of the organization and to become part of a purpose in which they participate. Once they are hired, of course, they have to fulfill a function, but their reason for joining should be the purpose.

The purpose of every endeavor should be to create an example of excellence in a community. Are you serving God, accomplishing His Will, pleasing Him and fulfilling His goals? Is it good for all concerned? Is it good for the employees and guests? Is it an investment in the community? Are you making a difference?

You should seek to answer all those questions honestly. If they can be answered yes, this endeavor should be pursued. In my conversations with Pastor Eric, he answered yes to all of those questions and I believe he has a model that more churches and non-profits should consider. Not only does his church serve the community with excellence, but they have also answered the question of sustainability and profitability.

How is a hotel good for the community? It fulfills a need by providing hotel rooms for people and allows people to connect. It creates jobs and hopefully within the jobs you are creating purpose for the employees. People work best in an environment of belonging and purpose. It is difficult to wash dishes and make up rooms. If employees are there only to perform those functions they cannot develop into leaders. They must have purpose and leadership has to give it to them. Servant leadership is highly professional. In the companies that I run we develop people into leadership roles more than management roles. You can give people technical training but giving them leadership ability is much more difficult. Management controls. Management forces you to do the job. Leadership creates an environment in which people like to do their jobs and believe that their contribution is vital.

The church should also be a place of leadership, service and hospitality, welcoming people into an environment that gives them purpose. The leadership of the church must give people a vision of what they can become. If churches do not have that mindset, there is something wrong with the church. That is expected of an excellent hotel no matter what market segment it is in. Shouldn't people expect the same from the Church?

When you live by strong spiritual concepts, you understand that you are serving the Lord in everything you do, whether you are serving guests or employees. The Church is criticized and told to move closer to the thinking of society and leave God behind, but as Christians that is impossible for us to do. When you have a relationship with the Lord you are better able to serve your community.

The Church has a chance to offer something that few organizations can provide—genuine love, care and service motivated by the love of Christ. The Church looks in the wrong direction when it looks to people and organizations for answers. Jesus said, "Seek first the Kingdom of God."[1] The Church should stay there. If you can enhance that by having a business, so be it, but you cannot separate the Kingdom of God from what you do in business. Government, industry, community and other non-profit organizations will discover that your successes are the result of the Christian values and godly principles to which every employee is aligned and upon which all your decisions are based. Then you will discover what real influence is about.

—Horst Schulze
Current President and CEO, The West Paces Hotel Group, Atlanta
Founding President and Former COO of The Ritz-Carlton Hotel Company

INTRODUCTION

THE IMPORTANT FOUNDATION

The nineteenth century minister and writer Andrew Murray cautioned his readers against placing too much trust "in men and money,"[1] when looking to the development and success of any mission.

I agree with Murray. Money is never anyone's savior. By way of explanation, I need to clarify up front that even though this is a book that encourages you to develop economic engines to further the work of your mission, the main emphasis of any mission is never to place an ultimate dependence on money.

Simply, money is a necessary tool that can be used for good. That's what this book is about. As wise leaders we need to learn how to develop economic engines and use them with prudence. This book encourages you in that direction.

A mission's success will ultimately depend on the principles it was founded on. In the case of faith-based missions, that foundation is Christ. I realize that people of faith and those who may not follow Christ will read this book and I welcome readers of all persuasions. I will tell you simply that I have found the hope that is in Jesus Christ and He is the foundation by which our non-profit organization and I aim to help the world.

This book is written in the spirit of 1 Timothy 6:17-19, which says, "Command those who are rich in this present world not to be arrogant nor to put their hope in wealth, which is so uncertain, but to put their hope in God, who richly provides us with everything for our enjoyment. Command them to do good, to be rich in good deeds and to be generous and willing to share. In this way they will lay up treasure for themselves as a firm foundation for the coming age, so that they make take hold of the life that is truly life."

It's my prayer that you will find and take hold of this life that is truly life.

**Act on the principles
of love and justice, and
always live in confident
dependence on your God.**

—Hosea 12:6 NLT

**From the days of John
the Baptist until now,
the kingdom of heaven
has been forcefully
advancing, and forceful
men lay hold of it.**

—Matthew 11:12 NIV

CHAPTER ONE

THERE IS A NEED

It's a familiar story: you're a leader in a non-profit organization and your group struggles from a lack of funding. What do you do?

It doesn't matter if your organization is a church, a camp, a missions group, a community outreach program, or an education or human services group the struggles are similar. Chances are your organization continually struggles to pay the bills. You're doing a good work, one that's helping people live lives of hope and promise, but funding is always tight. Sometimes bills get paid late. Staff members all have low salaries. Services and programs run the risk of being cut. There's never enough money to do all you want to do.

Perhaps your daily operations are funded all right, but you want to expand and you can't. You've got solid ideas and a cutting-edge vision for how things could look for your group in the future, but to travel the road between here and there, new revenue streams will be required beyond what your group is currently bringing in. Your organization could do so much more good, if only it could raise more capital.

Or perhaps your organization is bogged down from what I call the "Let's Be Practical" syndrome. The people making the decisions are not pessimists, (not exactly anyway), but they all tend to view your organization's mission through the reality of the budget. They say no to whatever good ideas come up because they've become "realists" (their word)—they've been around the block—and they know that the realities of funding prevent any organization from getting too wild with its dreams.

1

So what's the answer? How can your organization generate enough income to sustain daily operations and even look to the future? What would it look like if the almighty dollar wasn't the bottom line? What would it look like to dream again, to really envision what your organization could do if it had the capital it needed to reach people for good?

If you had a limitless stream of cash in hand, how might your non-profit go forward to continue doing great things?

VIVA LAS REALITY

I've experienced firsthand this tension between what an organization wants to do and what it can actually afford. When I first began working as a senior pastor in 1989, I dreamed some mighty big dreams for my "organization." I was really going to change the world and the non-profit organization I was called to lead—my church—was going to do some impressive things to help transform people's lives.

My wife, Rita and I were first called to a small church in the suburban community of Woodinville, Washington, right next to Redmond, the city of Microsoft, Bill Gates and all things up and coming. We were told that the people in this community were upwardly mobile; they represented a new corporate culture of young urban professionals who dreamed big dreams and did great things in new ways. With my entrepreneurial spirit and my wife's eye for details, we were surely going to fit in great. I envisioned explosive church outreach programs, dynamic community renovation projects, state-of-the art building projects, fully-scaled Christian education and discipleship programs. Things were going to be huge. We'd probably need to open a satellite campus soon, or at least expand into a larger auditorium.

God has such a sense of humor. When Rita and I pulled our Subaru hatchback into the graveled parking lot of our new assignment, what stared us smack in the face were two very plain, very aged and very small boxy modular units. That was the sum total of our church facilities. There was no landscaping out front, only scraggly dirt and weeds. I halfway expected tumbleweeds to blow by. A pathetic sign with faded letters, oddly announced the church's straightforward name: "Woodinville Church." (We would latter change the name to "New Life" with great hopes that it would be true.)

Inside was no more glorious. Rows of metal folding chairs were scattered about on a dirty, spotted carpet. Florescent lights buzzed like mosquitoes at a trout stream. The speakers for the sound system looked like they had been pulled out of someone's pickup truck. Everything looked old, small, worn out and very dated. (We found out later that our denominational administrators sent us to a church that they were planning to close soon, thinking rookies like us couldn't do much harm there.)

The people who showed up that first service seemed to fit right at home with the building's humble surroundings. Rita and I arrived early so we could meet everyone. The folks passing out bulletins had some missing teeth and didn't smell too good. A couple of people in the front row looked like moonshiners returning from a six-month-long hunting trip in the Ozarks. Shortly before the service started, someone pulled me aside to warn me that the pianist could become extremely agitated—literally slamming his fists on the keys and storming out—if I dared to make any on-the-fly changes to the song order, such as suggesting something as simple as, "Hey—why don't we sing the first and last verse only."

"Lord," I prayed silently, as I stood behind the small wooden pulpit for the first time. "Is this really your dream for this community? Is this really your plan for me?" I couldn't tell you how disappointed I felt. I was right out of seminary and ready to tear the world up for Jesus. Move over Billy Graham, here comes Eric Bahme—that's how I was feeling at first anyway—then, to come to this little old backward church of twenty people. Crash to the bottom. It was nothing at all of what I'd dreamed.

There was much work to be done. And, although I didn't know it yet, much of the good work to come would happen in my own life. I was the one who God would change. I was young and judging people and surroundings by their outward appearances only, but God was going to use this place of humble beginnings to shape and mold me in many positive ways. Fortunately, God gave me the grace to be patient and trust that He would use that little church in mighty ways.

The original congregants warmed up to us fairly quickly and us to them, the spark caught tinder and we quickly grew to about three hundred people. The building soon started to look more open and inviting. It even started to smell better. The piano player eased up whenever I suggested we try things a different way. By and large, the people in this church had caught the vision of what we could become.

Right away I wanted the church to grow and not just numerically; I had the good sense to want the church to grow in spiritual maturity, too. Part of that dream meant that we needed to become people who reached out to our surrounding community. We'd need to connect with the Microsoft corporate culture. Things around our backward church would need to change. We'd need to update our building, grounds and PA system. We'd need to hire a worship leader who could help us turn the corner to a more modern sound. We'd need to bring in a youth pastor and connect with families with teenagers. At the very least, we'd need to fix up the nursery and children's classrooms. All that was going to take faith—and money.

I knew there was much more we could be doing as well. One of the constant frustrations to me personally was that we didn't seem to be doing all that I felt God was calling us do. The majority of people in the church caught the vision, which was great, but having all those people on board also highlighted a tension: even though the implementation of our organization's mission of reaching people for the Gospel was beginning to be fulfilled, we could be doing so much more. We were being held back. When we dreamed together and looked around at the needs within our community, we saw the need for a counseling center, recovery programs and a larger facility for our own growing congregation. That was just scratching the surface.

The only model of leading this organization that I knew was the one I was doing, yet it wasn't working in many of the ways I hoped it would. A huge part of my task—undoubtedly my greatest task—was to train our church in spiritual maturity and helping the people in my care see beyond themselves to truly start serving the people around us. That was happening.

But fulfilling the dream would also take money.

And that was the big problem.

Try as I might, month-by-month the church still struggled. Sometimes we would do well and other times we would fall behind. While our giving was growing, it wasn't enough to keep up with our vision. We found land that we could buy for a new facility, but the church's vision was being held back by a lack of funds. Together, we had the faith to go forward, but not the capital.

What were we to do?

THE STRUGGLE TO FUND FORWARD

Our church wasn't alone in this struggle. As I networked with other pastors and non-profit leaders within the community, I often heard the same thing.

The traditional methods of raising funds for any non-profit organization included passing the plate, applying for grants and continually developing donor bases. But there lay the crux of the problem for us as a church—and it is also the crux of the problem for many non-profits today. All of these traditional methods depend upon one factor: encouraging people to give and keep giving. That one factor often proves to be the weakest link. Our church members in Woodinville were giving, but they were limited in how much they could give. Also, because our church was attracting new believers, a portion of the people were new to the idea of giving regularly, so they didn't fully understand the need to give consistently to an organization's operation.

Perhaps it's the same way with you. Funding an organization through donations only is always a limited vehicle. For instance, statistics show that for many organizations that rely on this vehicle, a minority of people will do the bulk of regular giving while a majority of people sit back and reap the benefits. The Barna Group recently reported that while as much as 65 percent of people make single contributions to a church during any given year, only about 9 percent of evangelicals regularly tithe to their church.[1]

Maybe the people you work most closely with will seldom, if ever, have any discretionary money to give; non-profits working with low-income people, teens, or children often face this problem. The very people who most closely see your organization in action or benefit from its operation often don't have the capacity to fund it themselves.

> The traditional methods of raising funds for any non-profit organization included passing the plate, applying for grants and continually developing donor bases. But there lay the crux of the problem for us as a church—and it is also the crux of the problem for many non-profits today. All of these traditional methods depend upon one factor: encouraging people to give and keep giving. That one factor often proves to be the weakest link.

Or maybe your organization depends heavily on grants and money that comes from foundations. Foundations are typically funded by seed money that's been invested, often in stocks, bonds, or mutual funds. If the economy dips, the initial investment goes down and less money is available for foundations to give and for organizations to receive.

Maybe your organization relies upon communication arms to get the message out to fund your vision. It takes money to get out there and reach potential donors. You've got to have money in order to bring money in—and ironically, you don't have the money yet to invest in fundraising.

No matter how the specifics emerge, the bottom line is always the same. When funding falls away for your non-profit, your non-profit suffers. Without funding, you lack the ability to sustain your mission. Programs need to be cut. New staff can't be hired, or existing staff members need to be laid off. New opportunities for direction can't be explored. The very people for whom your mission exists can't be served.

Unfortunately, I've recently seen several examples of this firsthand. At the writing of this book, America's national economy is in the midst of a severe slump. See if your organization can relate to any of these situations:

◆ A national evangelist depends upon his staff to make things happen. The evangelist is mainly an upfront man; his skills set lies in speaking and communicating the ministry of Jesus to large groups of people. His organization is small, just six people, but fortunately, he has hired well. His executive director's gifting lies in administration—the executive director runs all the daily operations of the organization. There are also bookkeepers, secretarial help and a capital campaign manager on staff who oversees fundraising for festivals. Unfortunately with a downturn in the economy, funding has suffered for more than a year now. Donations have fallen off and last month the board made the painful decision to lay off all the staff except the evangelist. Now, all his staff are out of work. The evangelist is also suffering because he can't do what he's called to do without his team of gifted people running the organization. A lack of funding has hurt this organization.

◆ A camp director has been tasked with overseeing the construction of a new dining hall. It's a strategic project and will mean the camp's mission of reaching kids in an outdoor setting can expand and look to the future. Unfortunately, the camp director will still need to run the camp while raising money for the new dining hall. His workload has doubled.

The camp's board would like to hire a fundraising specialist to oversee the capital campaign, but a lack of funds prevents this strategic move.

◆ A nearby church is experiencing explosive growth and needs to hire three more staff: a youth pastor for teens, a children's pastor and a worship leader. But most of the people in this church's congregation are new to the idea of tithing and the church can only afford to fill one of these positions. Church leaders are wondering how they will juggle this situation and meet their growing church's needs.

◆ A friend of mine recently retired from a lifetime of working in non-profit organizations. He told me that the highest salary he ever made was $30,000 a year. He and his wife had children to support and times were always hard financially, he said, although somehow they always made it. (At the time of this writing, an average family wage is about $50,000-$80,000 annually.) This man is well educated and has dedicated his life to helping people. Unfortunately, his salary barely paid for his family's needs, causing hardship in the family structure.

◆ Recently I saw on TV that one of the city's downtown shelters for homeless people is closing due to a lack of funding. The shelter's administration looked to the city government to supply its funding, but the government is not proving to be the answer in this case.

This is fact: Money is an integral part of any non-profit's forward thrust. Without money, it's difficult to operate, much less look to the future. Without money, the very thing your organization is called to do can't be done. When the giving goes down, it's easy to let a vision perish. How many times have you dreamed up an idea that's dependent on funding, but then the money isn't raised, so the project doesn't take off? As leaders, it can be easy to head down the road toward pessimism here. We become dangerous sorts of realists as we scale back our visions to fit with our organizations' incomes. Seldom do we fail to dream dreams, but frequently we grow frustrated and weary from trying to figure out how to fund them. We're forced to scale back because of what we deem as a lack of provision.

I want to offer a brief caveat here and say that there's nothing wrong with the funding mechanism of encouraging donations. Although this vehicle has its limits, it

> **This is fact: Money is an integral part of any non-profit's forward thrust. Without money, it's difficult to operate, much less look to the future.**

works; and we encourage, teach and practice tithing in the church I lead today. There is a significant blessing attached to giving and many people have yet to realize the power associated with faithfulness. But somehow, particularly in faith-based environments, we've come to believe that soliciting donations is the only way of taking care of an organization. Biblically, this would not be the case. The Apostle Paul was a tentmaker—he generated funds through a business. Priscilla and Aquila, a first century Jewish couple described in the New Testament, ran a business and funded their mission through that means. Even the Old Testament example of the Israelites moving from slavery into freedom and receiving the spoils of Egypt is an illustration of an alternative funding vehicle. Tithing is one good way. Yet we need to overcome the mindset that tithing is the only biblical way.

What if we were to really dream big and think outside the box? The God we serve is never short of cash. He invites us to ask Him for good things. Since God owns the cattle on a thousand hills[2] and since God invites us to continually merge our initiative with faith[3], how else might we fund our non-profit organizations, or fund them more effectively?

Dare to dream with me here. I'm not asking us to think up new ways to line our own pockets. There have been far too many abuses of that in the past. I'm asking us to always stay true to our values and our missions, to continually help people and continually work to transform people's lives and entire communities for goodness, faith and new beginnings, to dream up a new funding model that allows us to facilitate these good things. God has many plans that He wants to bless. The question becomes, are we open to exploring them?

Here's the very simple question that I first asked when things were developing in Woodinville; when it comes to generating funds for your non-profit organization, is there an alternative way?

REAL PEOPLE, REAL SOLUTIONS

The seeds that became the answer to this question were planted in me one day at an unlikely place. A good friend of mine worked as a programmer at Microsoft and he invited me to come to the campus one day for a visit. When I came to the campus that day in 1993, my friend showed me around the manicured grounds of one of the world's most profitable and powerful companies. Microsoft was already at the cutting edge of its mission and from the money its founder was bringing in, the company was able to do some amazing things.

After taking in the huge buildings, the new informal corporate culture and various examples of the impressive undertakings on campus, I said goodbye to my friend and headed back to my car. Pulling the keys out of my pocket, I hopped in and immediately felt God's presence welling up inside my chest. This was not the first time that I felt God's presence in a tangible way, but this time the feeling was overpowering. My heart pounded and my palms turned clammy with sweat. I sat still, my hands gripping the steering wheel. My legs went numb. My fingertips started to tingle. I lost the strength to move. I knew that a Power infinitely greater than myself had surrounded me. I waited with an enormous sense of anticipation. Every fiber of my being longed to hear what was coming.

Then God spoke. There was no audible voice, but God's words burned in my soul more clearly than if they had been spoken aloud. The question was simple and I knew immediately what it meant. God said, "Eric, what if Microsoft was a church?" In other words—what if a church was a multi-million-dollar corporation on the cutting edge of its mission? If I was the leader of an organization with virtually unlimited resources, what kind of radical community transformation would my organization be able to do? That's the same question I pose to you right now. If I laid down a check on the table in front of you for fifty million dollars, then asked you how your organization would spend it, what would your answer be? Think for a moment of some of the ways that amount of capital could help foster your organization's vision.

It was in that quiet moment in the Microsoft parking lot that for the first time I glimpsed how business (and the positive power of money) could be combined with a God-given vision to help people. When those two factors were joined, I knew that we could open doors to reach people in ways I had never dreamed possible. Suddenly I grasped a whole new paradigm where non-profit organizations such as a church could prosper instead of struggle. I caught a glimpse of a highly sustainable future. Instead of being locked inside a box with barriers, boundaries and a survival-mode congregation, I now had a new vision of a ministry without walls. A wave of emotion swept over me and tears streamed down my face. I knew that I had received a deeper call to action. I didn't have a name for it just then, but over time it would emerge as the Mission-Based Entrepreneur (MBE) model. The specifics for that model weren't all laid out that day in the Microsoft parking lot. Over the next years I would hone and craft this vision with the help of a team of like-minded partners. It's taken much time, prayer and energy to arrive where we are today. But what we've learned along the way is the very thing that I'd like to share with you in this book.

YOUR FORWARD PLAN

This MBE model is simple and straightforward, yet revolutionary: it's an invitation to fund your non-profit by pairing it with a business venture. This model recognizes that money is not the enemy; it is simply a tool. And that tool can be used for some powerful God-given initiatives.

In the MBE model, non-profit and profit ventures are combined with the common goal of championing your non-profit's mission. Your mission's original goals don't need to get lost. This model teaches you a way of funding your mission, but it's never for the intended purpose of becoming rich for money's sake alone. Simply "getting more money" is never the end goal. Money is only the means to help your mission succeed. The more capital you have, the more doors are opened to explosive new opportunities for life and ministry.

This model is one vehicle to radical community transformation. It gives you and your organization a new permission to rid yourself of pessimistic thinking. It allows you to see new tomorrows, new possibilities, new horizons—and then helps turn those visions into realities. Think of the MBE model as a pump that provides water on an ongoing basis. In the pages ahead we'll give you the tools to set up that pump and turn on the switch. Water will flow and keep on flowing! Do you have questions? A lot of them? That's okay. Most people do. Any time you're faced with a new paradigm, it's good to answer all your questions before putting that paradigm into practice.

Some people—particularly with faith-based persuasions—wonder if there's something sinful about combining business with mission. People sometimes misinterpret the Bible's teaching about money—that the love of money is the root of all evil[4]—as blanket teaching that we should avoid all money matters entirely. (Christ's specific command is to avoid a heart-level attraction to money allowing it to have first place in our lives. In other instances He notes that it is a tool to be used for goodness.)

Or perhaps it's because people view Christ's exchange with the money changers in the temple[5] as an injunction against merging business with God's house, when in fact, Christ's anger was directed at the misuse of money in the temple; the cheating of people that accompanied this specific practice of exchanging Roman coin for temple treasury and the overlooking of the poor and misfortunate that happened as a byproduct of this overemphasis of practice.

Other people will express an inherent mistrust about combining for-profit and non-profit ventures. Business people sometimes view those in the non-profit sector as out-of-touch, ignorant about how things operate, even unsophisticated about how organizations run. People in the non-profit sector sometimes view business people as greed-based or manipulative, where the money is always the bottom line. However, there's definitely a vision to be cast about the two groups coming together, understanding each other and working together for a common goal. Sometimes, non-profits can foster a poverty mindset, particularly in the church. Since we're in the business of helping people, often poor or needy, then we can't be too far removed from the people we're helping. Some have even convinced themselves that God wants the church and those who work for the church to be poor.

But already, in the secular realm, the concept of being a mission-based entrepreneur is being termed "social entrepreneurship." The concept is getting big attention—and big results.

Consider:[6]

◆ According to a recent Harris Poll, a whopping 97% of Generation Y are looking for work that allows them "to have an impact on the world." Today's next generation of brightest thinkers wants to combine business with mission.

◆ In recent years, courses or centers in social entrepreneurship have been created in over 250 universities and colleges such as Harvard Business School, Yale School of Management, Duke, NYU's Stern & Wagner, Wharton, Oxford and Stanford.

◆ Teach for America received 25,000 applications for 3,700 slots in 2008, an increase of more than a third over 2007. In Ivy League schools such as Yale, Cornell and Dartmouth, close to 10% of all graduates applied to the program. The trend of combining mission with business is strong and growing.

◆ In the past two years the Acumen Fund, an organization that supports social entrepreneurs who solve major problems through business solutions (e.g. malaria nets, water purification, loans for housing), received more than 1,000 applications from top ranked business students for just 15 fellowship positions.

The list of top business entrepreneurs who are focusing either full time or a considerable amount of time on social entrepreneurship is highly impressive, including:

◆ **Pierre Omidyar**, founder of ebay, who created Omidyar Network to "enable individual self-empowerment on a global scale."

◆ **Jeff Skoll**, cofounder of ebay, who also runs Participant Productions, which makes socially conscious films including "An Inconvenient Truth" and "Goodnight and Good Luck."

◆ **Bill Gates** has left Microsoft to pursue a full-time career in philanthropy.

◆ **Warren Buffett** recently donated $30 billion to the Gates Foundation.

◆ **William Draper**, one of the biggest venture capitalists in Silicon Valley, created the Draper Richards Foundation to support social entrepreneurs.

◆ **Klaus Schwab**, the founder of the World Economic Forum (Davos), founded the Schwab Foundation for Social Entrepreneurship.

- ◆ **Sergey Brin and Larry Page**, founders of Google, created Google.org, which supports social entrepreneurs and has raised over $1 billion.

- ◆ Legendary venture capitalist **John Doerr** is leading an effort to raise $100 million for microcredit loans.

This trend is already huge and it's increasing as we speak. And with good reasons—people want to be part of something that matters and they want to succeed in these ventures, even in hard economic times. MBE thinking can and will facilitate this.

I believe it's time to cast new vision for funding God's work. I believe the time is right for Christians to lead the way in mission-based entrepreneurial thinking. Merging business with mission creates sustainability and ultimately community transformation.

The MBE model is always about funding passionate and powerful dreams. Dreams that you can feel flowing through the veins of your soul; Dreams that you feel so deep, so inspiring, that you'll climb the hill, you'll go around the world, you'll roll up the sleeves of your faith and do whatever it takes to see them become reality. Several years ago, I was sitting in Horst Schultze's Mercedes while he was telling me about his dream of transitioning out of being the President and COO of the Ritz Carlton Corporation. Why would anyone leave this position of influence? Because he was dreaming of building a new chain of hotels—and this one would be the greatest six-star luxury brand of hotels the world had ever seen. "I will create the absolute best product worldwide," he said to me. And he meant it. That's passion!

This is what I want to help instill in you—a passion that drives your dreams! When funding is available, you no longer have to figure out how you're going to write the next grant, or beg the next donor for a buck. Instead, you can take that donor with a heart for your organization and set him on your board, or release him in other ways to help live out the dream.

Are you dreaming right now?

HOLD ON TO YOUR HAT

In the pages ahead, here is where we'll go:

First, we'll help you clearly define your mission. Before you launch into an MBE role, you need to know exactly what you are called to do in the inner core of your being. Your mission must come before money; first in time and first in priority. If you turn the formula around and seek money before mission, you're in trouble.

Second, we'll help infuse in you the ability to hold on and not quit, even when the night is dark. Following the MBE path is never easy. You will pay a price and we'll help you count the cost before you begin the journey. I love the imagery of Psalm 23 about how the Lord as our Shepherd leads us beside still waters. He anoints our heads with oil and our cups run over—this is an image of blessing and prosperity. But in the very same psalm He also leads us through the valley of the shadow. Are you prepared for the walk in the dark valley as well?

Third, we'll want to do some personal soul searching work. For some, this may seem like an unnecessary step, one that only slows things down but I've learned that if you're truly going to function as an MBE you need to deal with whatever's in your closet. Hidden fears, insecurities, moral struggles and emotional anxieties will bring you down unless you deal with them first. To survive as an MBE you need to have your priorities straight and your life clean. The MBE journey can be a rollercoaster ride and if you haven't dealt with the internal stuff you're going to unbuckle and fly off the tracks. Time and time again, history has shown this scenario to be true with everyone from Jim Bakker to Bernard Madoff. If you haven't first dealt with the inner woundedness of your life, the MBE process will result in death on the vine.

Fourth, we'll help you really dream, or dream again if your dream has long been stymied by the "Let's Be Practical" syndrome. This book will allow you to sort and pray things out and dream again.

Fifth, we'll do some work in the area of vehicle design. What kind of business will help you not only fund your mission, but actually *further* your mission at the same time? The MBE model always seeks complimentary relationships between business and mission. Will a storage unit help you make disciples? Will a thrift store help fund your camp? Will a strip mall help you reach the poor? For this book, the specific funding vehicle we're going to share in depth with you about is the hotel model, but there are plenty of other good ones out there as well.

Finally, we're going to give you a blueprint for becoming an MBE by showing you what we did. If you want to get into the hotel business, we're going to introduce you to a resource called the Christian Asset Network that will help you with many of the specifics of the plan. If not the hotel business, then we'll show you how to find and develop networks and alliances that will help you build your funding vehicle within your community. You can't do all of it yourself and you weren't designed to do it all yourself, but I bet you have people nearby your organization who can help. We'll show you how to partner with them by forming collaborative relationships—strategic partnerships that are a win-win for everybody.

So that's where we're going. Hang on to your hat, it's going to be a wild ride! Together, we're on the cusp of a movement, an MBE Revolution. It's not a movement that makes money for money's sake. It's a movement that gives it away.

This book promises to give you an answer to sustainability. You'll close this book and be able to realize your organization's dreams. That's what we've done with our church. We're not finished with the process yet, but we're on the other side. We travelled to a place where we were not afraid to dream and today we see those dreams being fulfilled, even better than we first imagined.

The funding challenges in front of any forward-thinking nonprofit organization are enormous today. But there is hope. Welcome to a new and innovative self-supporting ministry model based on solid business practice. This model will extend your ministry and mission to a broader reach while providing the proper and long term funding your mission requires.

Let's step forward boldly, together.

SUMMARY

+ The traditional methods of raising funds for any non-profit organization included passing the plate, applying for grants and continually developing donor bases. Traditional funding methods for non-profits are not wrong, but they tend to limit an organization.

+ Money is an integral part of any non-profit's forward thrust. Without money, it's difficult to operate, much less look to the future. Without money, the very thing your organization is called to do can't be done.

+ The time is right for Christians to lead the way in mission-based entrepreneurial thinking. Merging business with mission creates sustainability and ultimately leads to community transformation.

+ If you had a limitless stream of cash in hand, how might your non-profit go forward to continue doing great things?

CHAPTER TWO

THERE IS A SOLUTION

Although the dream to become an MBE was birthed inside me while I was in Woodinville, I never fully became an MBE while there. It took a shift of locations and jobs for me to fully step into this new paradigm. It may not be the same way with you. Perhaps you will become an MBE exactly where you are today. But for me, the change of locations and jobs was part of the process God was using to show me what it meant to become an MBE. I needed to learn more about this new way of looking at things before I could fully lay hold of what was to come.

In fact, a huge part of the learning curve came when I examined my own life, the type of man and leader I was and the talents and skills I brought to the table. I needed to develop the eight key characteristics of an MBE if I was ever going to succeed in this new arena. I've discovered that these eight character qualities are vital for success. When all eight of these qualities are fully developed and working maturely in a leader, they provide the necessary foundation to operate and thrive in this new role.

In this chapter and in chapters to come, I will share with you what we learned in those early years. By showing you what we discovered, maybe you won't make the same mistakes we did and you'll be that much more ahead. I don't mean to encourage you to rush the process in your life. Instead I encourage you to step boldly being well-informed and trusting that God will form these eight qualities in your life. Then, when the time is right you can walk into this new paradigm.

Here is part of our story:

A SINGLE STEP INTO THE UNKNOWN

Thirteen years to the day from the time my wife and I first drove our old Subaru into the parking lot of that little church in Woodinville, that chapter of our life came to a close. Things ended well. We loved the people we pastored, but we knew it was simply time to move on. My family and I would be moving about two hundred miles south to Portland, Oregon, for a new beginning.

We had not made this decision lightly. Here's where God's call to live by faith came into play again. I had a wife and a five-year-old daughter, Alyssa, to support, but no concrete offer of a job or a paycheck.

All we had was an opportunity.

In this case, our specific opportunity was to start a new church. Planting a new church is similar to starting a new business. It takes enormous amounts of time, energy and resources to get a new venture off the ground. Some people thought we were foolish! Why leave thirteen years as a Senior Pastor to start all over again? Sometimes we couldn't quite explain things to people when they asked us what we were doing. If you've never stepped out on faith, the process can seem foreign, even dangerous. But my wife and I were both convinced of the step we needed to take. God was telling us to move and when the inner push of the Spirit draws you to leave the only place you know as home, you have two choices—obey, or not.

> ...when the inner push of the Spirit draws you to leave the only place you know as home, you have two choices—obey, or not.

If you're a person of faith, you know that the Bible is full of examples that show this kind of faith in action. Gideon needed to stop looking at the small size of the army and focus on the huge size of God. Abram needed to leave his familiar homeland and go to another new, unknown land that only God would show him. The Israelites crossing the Red Sea with the Egyptian army at their back needed to splash in and get their feet wet before God parted the waters and let them pass on dry ground. Plenty of times throughout history people have been asked to begin a journey with a single step into the unknown.

If God is calling you to become an MBE you will face a similar journey of faith. The start of any new endeavor can be scary. You're being called to step out into the unknown. To jump without a solid plan of action.

Here's a fact for you; if you can't bear the thought of taking the first scary step of faith, you'll never make it through the middle. The first step may be tough, but the middle of the journey is almost always going to be harder. I won't sugar coat this for you. If you're going to become an MBE and merge your non-profit with a business, it won't be simple. But few things in life that are worth doing are easy when you begin. God uses such times to deepen your dependence upon Him and to let you know that it really isn't your abilities that will get the job done but His.

What I know from my experience, is that those hard steps along the way are part of the excitement in the journey. Once you near your destination and look back you know without a doubt that there had to be Someone greater than you leading you along the way. Your mission will be built on the solid foundation of God's provision. He's inviting you to step forward and depend upon His miracles. This is the type of exciting journey to which God invites us.

When we first arrived in Portland, God didn't miraculously offer me a paycheck. He didn't miraculously plant my church for us in a great location. God didn't give me a hotel or even the vision for one at first. We just got off the train and wondered what would come next. And the first thing God did was take me to school.

My form of "school" came from my interaction with a business-man named Torre Morgal. We gathered a small handful of people and began the church as quickly as possible. We passed the plate and collected offerings, but there wasn't enough money coming in to support me full time, much less rent a building or take care of the thousands of other expenses required to run a church. So I needed to become bi-vocational, doing the job of my mission virtually for free, while taking another job on the side to bring in income. Torre saw my need to go bi-vocational and offered me a job in hotel operations with his firm.

Thankfully, Torre became my tutor in the process of becoming an MBE and learning how to merge mission with business. Torre was (and is today) president and CEO of Lincoln Asset Management (LAM), a Portland-based privately owned hotel management firm with a reputation for progressive and successful property management. He was the first example I ever saw of a true MBE. By the time I met him, he already had years of experience and credibility in the hospitality industry. Torre was developing a strong network of dedicated professionals with extensive experience in hotel operations, sales and marketing, finance, technology and capital management. He bought hotels, built them and managed them successfully. He grew up in the business and had the respect of hotel franchise companies, brokers and bankers. Simply put, Torre knew people. And he knew how to get things done.

Going bi-vocational initially wasn't an easy decision for me. When Torre offered me a job in the hospitality industry, it was the first time I had worked outside my profession as a pastor. That felt very strange to me at first. I had always longed to be a pastor, always trained to be a pastor, always worked as a pastor. I knew that regardless of being in business or church, that calling to pastor would never leave. Yet this was unknown territory. How would I take my calling into the market place? It was all part of a larger plan for both Torre and me.

Have you ever found yourself in a similar situation? God opens a door that you know nothing about and asks you to step through it because He wants to teach you the things on the other side of that door. There can be a lot of trepidation at the idea of stepping beyond the threshold. I encourage you not to fear going through a door if it doesn't look like your calling. That door could be the very thing that releases your potential. For me, I had a vision from God for planting a church, the backing of my wife and the friendship and expertise of a well-credentialed businessman whose professional advice I could trust. I couldn't, however, see the big picture of how all three would come together to make my dream happen. Yet God knew exactly what He was doing. God was bringing about that dream through a process of friendship, education, training and relationships. He was teaching me things along the way I would have never learned otherwise.

> God opens a door that you know nothing about and asks you to step through it because He wants to teach you the things on the other side of that door.

It turned out that God had been working in Torre's life as well. Long before Torre ever met me, he was on the board of his church during a fund-raising campaign to build a new building. Every week the pastor came to the congregation—cap in hand—and asked for money for the project. Finally, when the church had collected enough seed money to begin work on part of the project, church leaders obtained a mortgage for $15,000 a month and started the work while the pastor continued to raise more money.

During that time, Torre's company purchased a hotel. As he studied the books, a light came on in Torre's head. His church—the same church he was sitting on the board of—was paying the exact same monthly amount for a mortgage on their new building that Torre's company was paying per month to purchase a hotel.

But the crazy thing was that a different church was renting meeting space in that hotel and paying Torre for the use of the conference room every Sunday morning and Wednesday night. Having a church in a hotel was proving to be a good thing. They had signed a contract to meet in the hotel for years into the future. This church was operating out of his hotel with no ill effects on the guests, which had been management's fear. Torre was receiving income from both the church and the hotel guests and those streams of income not only covered his monthly payment but also produced a profit that could be used to pay for other good things.

In contrast, Torre's home church was paying out money that went only to the bank. In his mind, this was a black hole. The new church building was vacant most of the week, while his hotel was bustling with activity every day of the week. Most of the people who attended church with Torre were already members there, so the church wasn't having much influence on the outside community. In the hotel, however, people from all walks of life came day and night and found a place of hospitality and warmth. They willingly paid money for the services the hotel provided and Torre could use the profits any way he chose.

This was the formula. His existing church needed donations and borrowed money to fund a building that was barely used, never generated income on its own and inadvertently sucked a great deal of funding from other areas that the church could use it for.

His hotel offered a meeting room (that was already being used by another church), the meeting room rental generated income, the hotel itself generated income and people who needed the very message the church provided were constantly on site.

The formula for success was coming together. We couldn't yet see how all the parts of the vision fit, but we had all the crucial pieces in place and they were beginning to click together.

The big question now, was how.

THE EIGHT ESSENTIAL QUALITIES

You may have your vision in mind. But God isn't giving you clarity on how it will all fit together. Or perhaps your dream is already well thought through, but for some reason there is a strange delay in proceedings. What's going on?

I could run a church. Torre could run a hotel. We were pretty sure that the formula for success meant merging the two. We were starting to grasp the specific vision, but things were still foggy. What—or more accurately, *Who* was slowing us down from jumping in?

God was.

I believe that God wanted us to learn eight essential qualities that would lay the foundation for making this new paradigm of merging business with mission succeed. I believe something similar will be true for your life. All of these qualities are interdependent. Just as every stone in an archway leans on its neighbor to maintain structural integrity, these eight principles depend on one another for support. God can develop all of them within you like He developed them in us. More than likely, it won't happen overnight. Success requires endurance on a small scale first.

As I examined these eight qualities of an MBE leader and how they were emerging in my own life, I saw the parallel in the life of the biblical character Joseph. It made sense. Joseph was one of the first true MBEs.

Developing these qualities slowed us down, yes, but they were vital to our success. I believe the same will be true for you. So let's take a look at these qualities together.

1. VISIONARY
The ability to dream—and keep dreaming

Many entrepreneurs, as children, had good imaginations and dreamed big dreams that seemed impossible to others but became their driving motivation. When Joseph was a boy growing up in Canaan, he was a dreamer and like many dreamers he faced opposition from the people he loved the most. He was particularly unpopular with his own family. His brothers mocked him to one another, saying, "Here comes that dreamer!"[1] Then they decided to kill him but later sold him into slavery instead.

Big ideas overwhelm people who lack the imaginative tendencies of MBEs. Joseph's dreams of success—seeing his parents and siblings bow before him—were too much for his brothers. His family should have become his closest friends and supporters, but they were not as open to new ideas as he was. Eventually he would be in a position to forgive his brothers and rescue them from death when his dreams came true. That's what entrepreneurs live for. Joseph was also young in casting vision and still had a lot to learn. As young as he was, he probably should not have shared his dream as overtly as he did—even his

> Big ideas overwhelm people who lack the imaginative tendencies of MBEs.

father told him he needed to calm down. Like many young entrepreneurs he may have been dealing with a little bit of arrogance and may have needed to learn a few more lessons. It's okay to develop these lessons along the way. Joseph had a dream initially, but that was it. The pit and the prison Joseph experienced would become part of God's plan to help shape the eight vital character qualities in Joseph's life.

MBEs release their imaginations to dream up new ideas that will help other people. They have a passionate desire to do things better. Often the fulfillment of their passion is even more important to them than the drive to make money, but when their ideas are good enough, wealth follows.

When Joseph arose from slavery and prison to a place of authority in Egypt, he was able to look at a problem—the coming famine—and create solutions along with efficient systems for implementing them. That was probably not the first famine to hit Egypt. However, Joseph was in a position of authority where he could implement innovations that came from years of trusting God through persecution and prison. He had the ability to see what others could not see. He could imagine a future where his "customers"—the starving people of Egypt and eventually his own family—would have things better because of his plan.

An MBE looks for a business model that will benefit a specific segment of the population and at the same time produce a profit for him. He lives with a sense that he is on the edge of a great adventure. He sees a particular area of frustration in society and lets his imagination roll until a solution is born. His focus is always on his customers and how he can meet their needs.

Because an MBE has a passionate desire to do things better for his customers, he is able to disregard nay-sayers who say it can't be done. He believes in his dreams more than he believes in society's definition of what is possible. He doesn't see the world as others see it. Everything seems possible to him, even in the face of impossible odds, especially if he has experienced the miraculous intervention of God, as Joseph did.

Joseph interpreted Pharaoh's dream and said it meant that Egypt was about to experience seven years of plenty followed by seven years of famine. He proposed a solution for Pharaoh to appoint commissioners to take a fifth of the harvest of Egypt during the seven years of abundance and store it. The food was held in reserve for the country so that the country would not be ruined by the upcoming famine.

When Joseph came up with this solution, he didn't put himself forward as the "discerning and wise man" to do the job. It looks like he had learned some valuable lessons along the way since he spouted off his dream to his father and brothers. Instead of saying, "Put me in charge and I'll fix things," Joseph offered a suggested plan for success, but it became obvious to Pharaoh that he had found his man.

2. RELIANT
The ability to seek God and inquire of Him

As strong, capable leaders, sometimes it seems counter-intuitive to be reliant on anything or anybody other than ourselves. But real MBEs know that God is the source of their success. They have learned to rely on Him to instill within them visions and dreams as well as provide the tools, resources and contacts necessary to develop practical skills to carry them out. They have personal habits of spending time with Him in prayer and listening to His voice. They learn how to discern between right and wrong in their business practices by studying the Bible. They believe that God has chosen and destined them to fulfill specific assignments that will benefit mankind and also cause them to prosper financially. Jesus said, "You did not choose me, but I chose you and appointed you to go and bear fruit—fruit that will last."[2]

Everywhere Joseph went in Egypt, he enjoyed success because he relied upon God. It didn't matter if he was running Potiphar's household as a slave, becoming a leader while inside the prison system or being second-in-command of the most powerful nation on earth. Joseph lived a blessed life. God wants to give that favor to His people today.

God's blessing marked Joseph's life. Everywhere he went, he prospered. That "luck" spilled over onto his employer, too. Things worked out for Potiphar just because Joseph was there. All Potiphar had to do was sit back and let his Israelite servant run the show. Joseph's life as a model prisoner blessed the prison system. He didn't carry resentment. He carried the Lord's blessings.

Often someone else reaps the benefits provided by the work of an up-and-coming MBE. For Joseph, it was Potiphar because Joseph served a master. Joseph managed an estate and the fruits of his labor benefited someone else. His time to lead the country had not yet arrived. He had to be faithful in one household first. In the same way, MBEs must be dedicated to excellence in small things before they arrive at their true calling. God is looking for men and women who will be faithful with "this" before He blesses them with "that." It is important to stay faithful in the place where God plants you—learning to steward the present before moving into the future.

There is an old saying that I believe is very true. The grass is not greener on the other side of the fence. The grass is green on the side where you water it. You must be content in the place where God has placed you before you can be released to a different location.

When you've truly learned what it means to be reliant upon God, then, when blessings come, you are able to avoid the natural tendency to get cocky and think you did it all yourself. You've learned that you are actually a passenger on the train of God's will.

3. HUMILITY
The ability to know it's not all about you

It's not all about you.

As strong, capable leaders we often think that it is.

But knowing and developing this one fact will help us further our mission with truth and real power. What we are creating is not for the sake of our personal kingdom but for God's kingdom. It's not all about us.

In Egypt, Joseph was a humble man who practiced humility as a lifestyle. He refused to pat himself on the back in front of the boss. Although he interpreted dreams that no one else could understand, he didn't leverage that into a drive for self-promotion. His goals were all about others—saving lives in Egypt. He offered a workable plan and asked for nothing in return. He didn't even ask to be released from prison.

MBEs have the ability to listen to God's voice and also take the advice of other people because they don't always have to be in charge. If something is not working for them, they can easily change. Joseph knew he would need one strategy for the times of plenty and another for the times of famine. MBEs look at all of the factors involved in staying on top of the market and are willing to adjust to changing times. That's what makes them successful.

MBEs stay updated on the latest technology and methodology so that they can make a market correction as soon as a new opportunity arises. They are not too embarrassed to ask for advice. They are willing to face the scrutiny and constructive criticism of board members and negotiate and compromise with employees when the circumstances dictate that they should. Humility gives them the right perspective on those in authority above them as well as those they supervise under them.

When MBEs fail, they are resilient enough to come back and succeed again because they have learned the power of humility. They have the ability to reflect on their reasons for failure and do things better the next time.

When you are humble, you are able to continuously learn new information. You are constantly exploring new ideas. Innovative MBEs often find themselves in the forefront of their industry. Since they are pioneers, they often hear people say, "It can't be done." If the reasons are right, they embrace them and make adjustments, but if the reasons are wrong, they disregard them in the right spirit and become successful where others failed in doing what couldn't be done.

If you insulate yourself from criticism and answer to no one but yourself, you will be tempted to do things that will eventually end in your downfall. Joseph understood that rejection and obstacles were integral to his learning on his path to power. He knew how to deal with his brothers appropriately in later years because he was humble. If he had been haughty and proud when he faced them, he would have been headed for failure. Instead he accomplished God's purpose.

> You must be content in the place where God has placed you before you can be released to a different location.

CEOs in today's business world who were making millions of dollars a year have fallen in recent months at an unprecedented rate. Their offices took up entire floors of skyscrapers littered with expensive artwork and designer furniture. Corporate jets shuttled them to business meetings with other CEOs in their ivory towers. They could take elaborate vacations and own multiple homes with all the trimmings. However, when they decided to remain aloof from course corrections they fell.

Jesus didn't build an organization and then refuse to listen to His Father. He didn't sit back and make others do the work. He was always in the forefront of His business. He interacted with the people, even tax collectors and prostitutes whom no one else would touch. Jesus was a man of the people, driven by His mission. As a leader, if you think you're too good for that, then you need to re-think your strategy.

I appreciate the humility of Horst Schulze who oversees the most successful hotels in the world. He also shows up at training sessions for employees. He rolls up his sleeves and picks up trash in the lobby if it needs it. He greets every person he meets as an important person, no matter if the person is a VIP or a janitor.

Some people see leadership as a pyramid with the CEO on top, the undisputed king of the hill. Then underneath are the VPs, then the division leaders and so on, all the way to the bottom where the minimum wage, entry-level grunts work to move the business forward.

I don't believe in that model. In fact, I see it as just the opposite. Yes, leadership is a pyramid, but an *inverted* pyramid. The leader is at the bottom, in the point of the triangle, with the whole organization on top of him. It's all about accountability and service.

An MBE in a leadership role must be accountable for every person he leads. If you're in charge of a team of five, you're carrying those five on your shoulders. If you're in charge of an entire organization, you're responsible for every single worker. Leadership is a calling that cannot be taken lightly.

In the beginning of our ministry, Rita and I pastored a small church. Today, we are blessed with a larger church. We are pastoring one of the fastest-growing churches in the Portland area and lead a significant business in a dynamic, paradigm-shifting industry. The tables have turned. Now people come to ask us what we're doing that is generating so much growth. I struggle to answer that question if people aren't able to see things from a faith perspective. I know we are doing some things right, but I really do sense that I'm simply along for the ride on God's train.

You, too, can follow this new model, but if God's call isn't the driving force behind you, nothing will happen. I used to go to large conferences and come back to my church and try to implement what another church was doing in hopes that I would get the same results. It never seemed to work for me. A true MBE knows in the core of his being that God is the driving force behind the ministry, not just progressive ideas. He recognizes the frailty of each moment and understands that whatever God has established for one day can indeed be gone the next.

It's easy to be humble when you know it really isn't about you.

4. HONESTY
The ability to do the right thing—even when it hurts

Joseph was a good-looking foreigner whose appearance attracted the attention of the woman of the house in Egypt where he worked. This created a problem because she was his master's wife. Joseph could have compromised and succumbed to her advances, reasoning that Potiphar would never find out. After all, his master trusted Joseph completely.

However, because Joseph was trustworthy and an honest man he refused her. When he denied her advances, her rage at being scorned led to her false accusation and his imprisonment.

"But he refused. 'With me in charge,' he told her, 'my master does not concern himself with anything in the house; everything he owns he has entrusted to my care. No one is greater in this house than I am. My master has withheld nothing from me except you, because you are his wife. How then could I do such a wicked thing and sin against God?' And though she spoke to Joseph day after day, he refused to go to bed with her or even be with her."[3] Although no one knew he was innocent, God honored him and eventually promoted him to one of the highest positions in Egypt—far above his former master who had imprisoned him.

This temptation turned out to be a pivotal moment in Joseph's life. What would have happened if he had given in? Potentially, the affair might have been kept a secret. Joseph might have lived a long and prosperous life in Potiphar's household. But the greater plan might never have been realized. Could it be that he would never have become a ruler? Would his family have starved in the famine? Would Israel not have become a nation? We don't know the answers, because Joseph made the right decision.

The two biggest reasons for failure in leadership today are sex and money. Both stem from unchecked lust and greed—chinks in the armor of integrity. Joseph responded to the woman's advances, "I can't do that. It's a sin against God." Your attitude should be the same. Joseph didn't give in. He never forgot his mission. He knew what he was supposed to do. It's easy to compromise

> The two biggest reasons for failure in leadership today are sex and money. Both stem from unchecked lust and greed—chinks in the armor of integrity.

when the pressure is on, but an MBE understands the bigger picture. Keep the right focus—on God and people, not wealth and power and let God promote you.

The challenge to Joseph's integrity came when he was on his way to a promotion. He just didn't know it was coming. I don't believe that was a coincidence.

It's easy to cut corners when the pressure is on; to say, "No one will ever know." But in so doing, you stall your potential advancement. Stay vigilant and don't be tempted to compromise your standards. You are in a race and you are on your way to a great victory. Strong moral character and integrity are no guarantee of worldly success, but with them you will be able to run well. Without them, your achievements will be worthless.

Joseph knew he had received a sacred trust from his master. I know I have received a sacred trust to care for the people who come to the church and the hotel. Today, we know that we cannot compromise our values; for instance, hotels today make significant amounts of money from providing in-room pornographic movies. Some companies refuse to remove them from the lineup of channels because of the high demand and high profits. Sadly, I know of hotels and hotel chains owned by Christians that refuse to remove the pornographic channels because of the income this filth generates.

At our hotel, we don't offer porn and we never would!

It's as simple as that.

We are under contract with our franchise to offer one premium channel, so we offer the HBO Family channel and our customers are also able to watch the regular lineup of cable stations—we don't attempt to regulate those or offer input into their decision making. But as far as it depends upon us, we will not offer in-room pornographic movies. Certainly, we generate less money because of that decision. But we will not participate in ruining families or the integrity of others.

That's the right thing to do.

That's what it means to be honest.

5. RESPONSIBILITY
The ability to have others depend upon you as you offer your best

When you're an MBE, you accept full responsibility for each new venture. Even when no one is looking, you maintain the same commitment to excellence, from small details to large. You do the right thing because others are depending on you.

Joseph was the image of responsibility. He was so good at his job that the only daily decision his boss had to make was what to eat for breakfast. With Joseph around, there wasn't a thing for Potiphar to be concerned about.

Whether you're running a hotel or a church, you take whatever resources you have and squeeze everything you can out of them to be a responsible owner. You buy the best seats for your congregation, install granite countertops in the bathrooms and replace every burned-out light bulb.

When we hire employees at Eastside, I always sit down with them before their first day of work. I tell them that if they're looking for a regular 9-5, then Eastside isn't the place for them. I also ask them what they would do if they saw a piece of trash in the parking lot. No one is too big to pick up a candy wrapper and this shows personal responsibility to the mission.

This is a business where employees take ownership in what they are doing. We are responsible to God for this ministry. We're not doing it for the money. As my nephew Brian has shared with many guests who apologized for not having any cash for a tip—"I don't do this job for tips. I do this job because I want to serve."

Nothing we do belongs to us. This is God's hotel.

Christ said that whatever you do for the least person you are doing for Him.[4] When you genuinely strive for excellence, you imagine that everything you do is a service to the King. It doesn't matter if you're in church seats or not. You keep it new and the best way to do that is to take responsibility for the details.

Walt Disney wanted Disneyland to stay new, to be always sparkling and fresh. He intended to give his visitors the same feeling of happiness every time they came. That meant keeping the grounds immaculate, painting buildings several times a year and opening new rides every season.

On the surface, pouring so much of your profits back into your business doesn't sound like a winning business proposition, but Disney had a vision greater than another run-of-the-mill amusement park. He created brand recognition that changed the world as a result of taking responsibility for details.

6. FOCUS
The ability to keep the goal in mind—always

From Joseph's story, it's very clear that he made a profit. He was focused on a mission that would help people, which should always be our goal. Yes, he built up personal wealth and power. He grew a dynamic organization that sold grain to the rest of the world when the market value of his product skyrocketed.

The Bible records the result as this: "Joseph collected all the food produced in those seven years of abundance in Egypt and stored it in the cities. In each city he put the food grown in the fields surrounding it. Joseph stored up huge quantities of grain, like the sand of the sea; it was so much that he stopped keeping records because it was beyond measure."[5]

Yet Joseph never forgot his focus to help others before himself.

MBEs know that abundance will come because of their dream to help others. They are focused on the value of their dream. They believe that their business idea will succeed and will someday make their organizations prosper if they apply themselves now. Their thoughts are dominated by the dream. Their time management decisions are made on the basis of their destiny.

Great entrepreneurs make a daily commitment to stay customer-oriented instead of self-oriented. MBEs make a commitment to put people and the mission first. When you're an MBE, you see beyond money or even a good product or service to your mission. There's nothing wrong with going from prison to a palace as Joseph did. There's nothing wrong with going from rags to riches, but true success comes by remaining focused on the real goal. Paul said to keep your eyes on the prize of God's high calling.[6]

At Eastside, keeping this focus is especially important now that we bring in millions each year in gross revenue with our ministry. Our mission remains focused on the high calling of helping and serving people. The byproduct is that we receive money, so we take that money and pour it back into our mission. We're always looking for new ways to give back, whether it's through state-of-the-art housing for the homeless, job training, English as a second language (ESL) programs, collecting food for other shelters or running a recovery program. Along the way, we're also looking for new ways to make money. We're not afraid of success because the more we make, the more we can give back.

Joseph wasn't merely a great leader. He was also a great businessman. His ideas for business were focused. He knew exactly what to do to be successful. Even though he had been a slave and a prisoner, each time God opened up opportunities he proved to be an excellent manager. He demonstrated godly character.

When Pharaoh offered Joseph that huge promotion, the Bible doesn't record that he was fearful or resistant. When you're not afraid of success, you can reach out and take it when the opportunity comes your way. You can seize your opportunity.

When you have a passion for making things happen, you don't sit around waiting for opportunities to come your way. You aggressively go after them. You make them happen—secure in the promises God has made to you. You take on a task and you focus on completing that task, with excellence. You follow through on testing and product safety. You take the product all the way to market. You are moving and full of energy, never stagnant. Your enthusiasm and focus attract others, especially if you're practicing the character traits we have been describing for an MBE.

7. PERSISTENCE
The ability to keep going, particularly when the way gets hard

Opposition comes to every visionary, so there will be times when you have to persist in the midst of great obstacles. Joseph was thrown into a pit and sold into slavery by his brothers. His employer's wife falsely accused him of rape and he spent years in prison. Perhaps your obstacles won't be that severe, but they will come, nonetheless.

At Eastside, we've had many obstacles to overcome. Before we bought the hotel, we were broke. After we bought the hotel, we were not only broke but bleeding. Little did we know that those were not the biggest hurdles we would face. That was only the beginning.

In order to become a successful MBE, you have to be resourceful. You look at every hurdle as something to leap over in the midst of the race. If you're not too good at going over the hurdles and they keep tripping you up, you learn to go around them or under them.

Competition requires persistence. Regardless of your product or service, someone will offer something similar, but your goal is to offer the best. You persevere. You do whatever it takes to come out first.

Every MBE needs patience along with persistence. Joseph had dreams that did not immediately manifest. He stayed in prison for two extra years until the man he had asked to speak to Pharaoh on his behalf finally remembered his charge.

MBEs run an endurance race, not a sprint. Sometimes you will see a challenge before you and you can either press through or give up and quit. That's when you find out if you are built to last.

> Opposition comes to every visionary, so there will be times when you have to persist in the midst of great obstacles.

I get calls from people all over the country saying, "Eric, it's great to hear what you're doing in Portland. We want to do the same thing over here! We're going to go get our own hotel, too!"

That's great. I love their enthusiasm, but one thing is certain. Times will come when you're stuck in a pit, like Joseph and you have to ask, "Is this working? Can I endure this any longer?" Every venture is a risk, but every great risk produces even greater rewards. If you let people dissuade you from taking risks that you know are necessary, you will not succeed. You must be willing to be ridiculed and criticized and not give up, because you can see the road ahead better than those around you.

When you're on the leading edge of change, everywhere you go you encounter stress. You are a pioneer going where few have gone before. You need to learn how to handle stress so that it will not rob you of the energy you need to press on. For me, stress relief is my home where I go to find peace and love. It's a church where people love one another like a family and we are going forward with the dream together. I get tears in my eyes so often when I see the faces of the great people we have at Eastside. They inspire me to press on. I love them so much. These people just don't quit.

My greatest stress-reliever is time alone with God in my private study at home where I can unburden myself to Someone who understands all about me and called me to this dream.

8. GENEROSITY
The ability to give—and keep giving

The eighth and last character quality of an MBE is generosity. In some ways it is the first quality, because it demonstrates the great commandments—to love God and love your neighbor as yourself.[7] Joseph had every right to refuse to help his brothers. In fact, he could have had them killed for showing their faces in his domain. They had betrayed him, sold him into slavery and given him up for dead. The last thing they deserved was mercy. However, instead of retaliating, Joseph showed them forgiveness and generosity. He showered his family with love and lavish gifts.

Joseph insured his family's survival through the remaining years of famine by inviting them into his kingdom and supplying all their needs. Instead of meeting them with anger, he gave them a haven of safety.

God loves a cheerful giver.[8] He always blesses givers. When you put others before yourself and are willing to sacrifice on their behalf, you are most like God. The heart of God is the heart of a giver. The core of His being is giving. He searched all of heaven to see what He could give to mankind and then He gave His only Son.

The Bible says clearly that nothing we have is our own.[9] Since we don't own anything, we should not have a problem giving it away. Everything we have came to us as a gift from God. God gives us the Earth as our inheritance because it is. He owns it all. Our possessions are on loan for us to use for an appointed time.

One of our families' personal goals, similar to what R.G. LeTourneau did, (a true MBE who lived from 1888-1969; he made large sums of money in the manufacturing sector and then founded LeTourneau University and LeTourneau Christian Center), is to reach the point where we can give away 90 percent of our income and live off of 10 percent. Rita and I aren't there yet, but we're pushing toward that goal. It's not necessary for success and maybe you won't feel that same call on your life. That's okay. But I do know that one characteristic of MBEs is generosity and no one can out-give God!

YOUR NEXT STEPS, TODAY

As you have read over these character qualities, I hope that you have seen yourself and these qualities being developed in you. If not, have the courage to conclude that becoming an MBE perhaps isn't your calling—or at least, not yet. Understand that God is the one who can and will form these traits in you if you have a willing heart. It might seem like a lot, but this path isn't for everyone. We always want to be very upfront about that.

But maybe these qualities describe you. You've seen them in action in your own life and you're excited to press on. Once you've examined your life and motives against the checklist in this chapter, we'll encourage you to dream big—to release the MBE inside of you. That's what we allowed ourselves to do when dreaming of the possibilities of our venture. That's what we'll talk about in the pages to come.

SUMMARY

✚ A key part of the learning curve in becoming an MBE comes from examining your own life first and making sure you're the type of leader who's up to the challenges of running both a mission and a business.

✚ Success begins from first developing eight key character qualities. When all eight of these qualities are fully developed and are working maturely in a leader, they provide the necessary foundation to operate and thrive in this new role. Developing these qualities will slow you down a bit, yes, but they are vital to your success in the future.

✚ The eight vital qualities of an MBE are:

1. **Visionary:** the ability to dream—and keep dreaming.
2. **Reliant:** the ability to seek God and inquire of him.
3. **Humility:** the ability to know it's not all about you.
4. **Honesty:** the ability to do the right thing, even when it hurts.
5. **Responsibility:** the ability to have others depend upon you as you offer your best.
6. **Focus:** the ability to keep the goal in mind—always.
7. **Persistency:** the ability to keep going, particularly when the way gets hard.
8. **Generosity:** the ability to give—and keep giving.

CHAPTER THREE

ALLOW YOURSELF TO DREAM BIG

Elephants.

They're gray. They're wrinkly. They're slow. What could elephants possibly have to do with developing economic engines that drive MBE movements?

Let me explain ...

I once read something about the training techniques for elephants that was vitally important in helping me understand the difference between staying inside the box as a frustrated leader and breaking out into the new thing that God had prepared for me. It's said that a strong adult elephant will not move if a piece of twine is tied around his leg and attached to a simple twig. That is how elephant owners in Asia keep them from running away. Why don't the elephants run? With nothing more than a simple tug they could find their freedom. It would be so simple for the huge pachyderms.

The answer is that they just don't know enough to change an old mindset.

You see, when elephants are small, they are first chained to large objects such as trees. They pull and pull all day and never make the tree move. So eventually they accept their fate and give up. When they are grown, the feeling of the tether on the leg tricks them into believing they are still chained to something immovable, even if it's only a piece of twine to a twig.

Leaders can be like that, too. It is not the twine around their leg that keeps them from walking through the door of opportunity. It is the chain around their mind.

The world—or even your colleagues or people close to you—chain you by saying this is all you can do. You stay tied to a model that says passing the plate is the only way you can raise funds. You stay tethered to a false sense of protection and security or by the fear of the unknown.

> Leaders can be like that, too. It is not the twine around their leg that keeps them from walking through the door of opportunity. It is the chain around their mind.

When I was a younger pastor, I didn't realize that many of the pastors in my former denomination and I were headed toward a future that resembled an elephant on a string. God had spoken to me about moving forward with my dreams for transforming a community. He had empowered me by the Holy Spirit but I kept running into people who tried to keep me tied up by fears, rules and traditions.

As the technology boom in the Northwest built success upon success, not only did the economy change, but also the way people lived. We had an expectancy of greatness. You didn't have to work at Microsoft, Amazon or one of the other technology giants to catch the enthusiasm of the dreamers.

I had a vision as big as Microsoft. I knew that if I stayed tethered by the twine when God wanted me to be released, I was in danger of becoming nothing more than a plodding cargo carrier, once strong and vital but now anemic and irrelevant.

If God has placed within you a vision as powerfully as how He spoke to me at Microsoft, let Him develop you before you forcefully tear the twine that binds you and then boldly cross the threshold of your opportunity.

Waiting patiently is important in this stage. God will invite you to a new liberty when the time is right. Listen to the voice of God in your life, then when the time is right, snap that false chain and break free! A whole new world of opportunity awaits you.

AN EXPANDED VIEW

I can't stress enough the importance of waiting until you know that God is telling you the time is right to break free. Until that time, work on honing and crafting your dream so you'll be able to hit the ground running.

When God gave me a bigger dream for my life and ministry, He didn't immediately take me out of my situation in Woodinville, but all the time I was there I kept dreaming. The knowledge that something greater was coming helped me to be patient. I saw life filled with possibilities. Even if the great deeds that I had dreamed about were not yet realized, I could at least see that if they became fully funded, they could become reality. If I were the

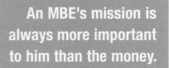

An MBE's mission is always more important to him than the money.

pastor of a church with the resources of Microsoft, we could provide practical solutions to real human needs. I knew that a business as big as Microsoft led by a pastor could sustain a ministry so large that we could help others in many extraordinary ways.

The dream I began to hone was of a revolution where entrepreneurs dreamed of helping people. The name for this revolution came to me as I began to write out the details of this dream within these chapters. You've heard it all through this book already. Instead of a leader whose distinctiveness was built around his MBA, I would become a leader whose drive came from his purpose—a Mission Based Entrepreneur or MBE, as we've mentioned. I dreamed of not only becoming savvy in economics, but also a "master of missions." I wanted to fulfill a purpose greater than myself.

I mention this again because in this chapter, along with casting a broader scope for dreams, I also want to further define the term MBE for you. The two concepts go hand-in-glove. Like a businessman with an MBA, an MBE dreams of making money—this is true. We don't ignore money, we dream of making it. But with one major difference! An MBE's *mission* is always more important to him than the money. A true MBE never forgets what drives him. He is driven by the desire to fund his mission and help people. An MBE makes money that he knows he will never get to spend because he receives such great fulfillment from spending it on others. Mission-Based Entrepreneurs understand that their mission to help others is the call of their destiny. It keeps them awake at night. It drives them to make a difference in the world.

A true MBE develops his dream while keeping his view of money in its proper place. An MBE may create much money within his career, but he always lives in confident dependence on God—not on the money that flows through his organization. He governs his life, his ministry, his business enterprises and his role in his community according to biblical principles of love and justice.[1] He can be rich in faith and his organization can be rich in goods, but he always keeps his priorities straight.

Yet, this is equally true within this expanded definition: being an MBE—including the role of being a pastor or Christian leader—does not mean that your organization (or even you personally) needs to be poor. It does mean that you have to be righteous, but you can be righteous and financially solvent.

When the Bible describes a Christian leader or pastor, it lists character qualities such as being above reproach, being "self-controlled, respectable, hospitable, able to teach, not given to drunkenness, not violent but gentle, not quarrelsome."[2] It also talks about money, love of family and a good reputation.[3] When the Bible describes a leader as "not a lover of money,"[4] that doesn't mean that a leader cannot possess money himself. I recognize this is potentially dangerous teaching, so let's unpack this a bit:

Historically, churches have often practiced the maxim, "you can't love what you don't have," and then aimed to "protect" its pastors from loving money by making sure they don't have any. I believe this is the wrong approach. The same Christian businessmen in the church who have no qualms about acquiring money for themselves can't seem to offer their pastors that same opportunity to prudently acquire and then use money for good purposes.

Money isn't intrinsically good or evil unless it keeps a person away from God. Some leaders are called to a life without worldly goods, but not all of us. We need to overcome the poverty mentality within the Church that says that all money is bad. There is nothing wrong with money. It is not the root of all evil. The love of money is evil. Excellence in business ventures should lead to profitability, which for an MBE produces a greater ability to give money away to finance good works.

It's true that Jesus told one rich young ruler to give away all he had,[5] but notice that Jesus didn't give the same advice to everyone He met. That young man loved money too much and it was interfering with his ability to follow God. It's not the same for everybody. For instance, the Bible says that when the righteous prosper, cities rejoice.[6] We see the tangible results of that verse with our hotel-church. City officials in Portland, Oregon, rejoice that the owners of the Quality Inn and Suites and Rodeway are prospering, (trust me, the city loves taxes). As a result of our prosperity we are able to bless the city with good works and tax revenue. When God gives His people wealth and they use it well, that sign of God's blessing and good stewardship makes an impression on the surrounding community.

So let's look at a few specific ways an MBE can correctly view and manage money. An MBE needs to use money well, personally and corporately. Some of the same biblical passages that are (falsely) used against pastors and other mission-based leaders to keep their salaries low actually indicate the opposite. God invites many of His people doing His work to experience the blessings that can come from financial solvency.

Below are several examples of how an MBE uses money:

1. To manage well his own family

A Christian leader needs to manage his family finances and provide money for his family's needs as well as giving them love and spiritual oversight. His wife will be a lot happier if she doesn't have to worry about when the next paycheck will come in or whether their small paycheck will be enough. I've heard preachers' kids say things such as, "I don't want to go into pastoral ministry because I don't want my kids to have to go through what I did. I want to be able to provide for my family financially." This is a legitimate concern.

2. To pay his household bills on time

1 Timothy 5:18 says "Do not muzzle the ox while it treads out grain." The idea is that provision needs to come from work. Some pastors quit the ministry because they can no longer live with the stress of being unable to pay the ordinary expenses of daily life. You don't have to love money to want enough money in the bank to cover your family's basic needs before the bills come in the mail. Pastors should be able to save for the future and send their kids to college. Why should a pastor have to rely on weddings and funerals or take a second job just to break even? Does that stressful lifestyle accurately represent God and the Kingdom of God? Is that a fulfillment of the Bible's admonition to honor church leaders? 1 Timothy 5:17 indicates that church leaders who oversee congregations are worthy of "double honor." I believe part of that double honor means that pastors should be paid well, not poorly.

3. To be hospitable

Like it or not, it often takes money to practice the ministry of hospitality. Leaders who work for the church or other mission-based non-profits should never have to be concerned about how they can take guests out to dinner at a quality restaurant or entertain them properly in their homes. The Bible says, "Do not forget to entertain strangers."[7] That applies to pastors, too.

4. To move freely in a secular leadership culture

This is a fact of life today: city leaders in government and the private sector typically don't view a pastor or non-profit leader as their equal if he wears a frayed shirt or drives a rusty sub-compact car. They may respect his good deeds, but they won't see him as their equal as a city elder[8] unless he can dress and drive within the norms of a leadership culture. Specifically, (depending on a city or region's culture) this will mean wearing quality suits, shirts, shoes and a watch or business-friendly casual attire and driving a family-based or corporate-looking car or SUV that is consistently washed, maintained, undented, non-rusty and about six years old or newer.

I mention that about cars carefully, as cars can become emotionally-charged items. Yet if you're a church or non-profit board member reading this and if you have a trusted relationship with your pastor or non-profit's director, I invite you to prayer-fully examine the car he drives. If it's a piece of junk, encourage him to take his rightful place as a respected community leader and buy or lease a newer one. In your role as board member, you may also need to help secure additional funding to make this a reality. Invite your church or nonprofit organization to consider leasing cars for your staff as corporate expenses or incorporating transportation expenses into salary packages. If we expect our leaders to be taken seriously in secular culture, we need to help them look, act, dress and drive the part.

When you are an MBE earning money that you use to help the community, you gain respect from providing needed services to your city. No longer is your church or organization isolated. You have now become a contributing part of your community. Your due diligence has created a self-funding missions model that sustains your dream regardless of church growth or the size of your congregation or organization. That's a win-win for everybody.

5. To reach people

For an MBE, this is the primary importance of making money. I purposely placed this point last on the list because with altruistic drives we often forget our personal needs (the ones I've mentioned above).

When you earn business profits that you can designate to the outreach of your mission, you have tapped into a sustainable funding source and you can also broaden your reach. Your organization can make an even greater contribution to society beyond what could be accomplished with donations alone. You have the ability and the funding to provide jobs and feed the poor, rescue the homeless and rehabilitate criminals.

We've seen many tangible results of this principle in action. In the church-owned business I pastor now, the congregation is able to hold its meetings in the hotel conference center. Church members, students and people in the community who need jobs can work in the hotel business while it is making money for ministry. We have additional funding to care for the needs of the poor, help the addicted and support missionaries around the world because money comes in from travelers every night. These guests love our customer service that is empowered by our faith.

The dream is working.

GIVING WINGS TO YOUR DREAM

Okay, with that undergirding of financial know-how in mind, let me ask you a question: how's your specific dream doing? Is it strong in your mind right now or is it still being developed? Is it forgotten and near-dead in the recesses of your memory, something that's been squelched out of you by the elephant trainers?

I know in my own life that my vision has gone through many stages. Sometimes it's been nearly dead or non-existent, sometimes it's gone through periods of waiting, shaping or crafting and other times it's been strong, actualized and vibrant.

In the early 1990s, shortly after I had begun pastoring the church in Woodinville and before I found myself in the parking lot at Microsoft, I learned a lesson about establishing the right spiritual foundation before God could trust me with His vision for my life. Early one morning, I awoke with a strong desire to pray and read the Bible, so I got out of bed and went to my study. As I read the words written centuries earlier by the prophet Jeremiah, a sentence leaped off the page: "'For who is he who will devote himself to be close to me?' declares the Lord."[9]

God seemed to be asking me, "Eric, will you be a man who will devote yourself to be close to me?" This was not a casual moment. God was presenting me with a covenant and He expected a response. Like the "I do" at the altar in a wedding, this commitment would forever change my life. There were no musicians, no choirs, no angelic voices. It was just God and me in a simple moment of truth when He asked me. "Will you take me to be your God?"

The moment with God at Microsoft that came later would release me to follow a bigger dream, but in this early morning moment God was presenting me with the question not of what I would follow, but Whom I would follow. It wasn't a salvation moment. It was an allegiance moment. He was asking for my devotion. God had given me His vision for my life—absolute devotion to Him—and I said yes.

Once the issue of my devotion was settled with God, He could begin to prepare me for what would come. His preparation included my personal change. The Bible says that we have a corrupt nature that shows up in self-centered arrogance, especially against God. Our human nature wars against our spiritual nature. God has to kill it off in order to release the power of His Spirit. That's when we really come alive to accomplish great things. That's when, as the Bible says, "I no longer live, but Christ lives in me."[10]

Before God gave me that big dream of being an MBE, I had already acknowledged that I was helpless without Him. I knew I needed Him for everything. I could do nothing on my own. I was convinced that whatever success I would have in the future would be a result of God at work in me. That is easy to say but difficult to work out and it doesn't just happen overnight. At times it would become painful as I lived out the dream of a business-ministry merger as an MBE.

Then, after I left Woodinville, I began to pastor a church while working in the hospitality industry with my friend Torre for Lincoln Asset Management. The dream that God had given me that day at Microsoft was strong in my mind, but now it seemed a long way off. Little did I know that God was doing some strong work within me to help shape and hone my dream.

One night early on in the beginning days of Eastside I was lying in bed reading a book called *The Celtic Way of Evangelism* by George G. Hunter III that described the life and times of St. Patrick and the many churches that he planted. Suddenly, I was struck with another one of those divine moments.

Most people don't realize that St. Patrick was one of the most effective evangelists of his day. Patrick and the other Christians with him launched a revolutionary outreach movement that succeeded at spreading the Gospel (their mission) in profound ways, primarily by meeting people's practical needs. They planted hundreds of churches within monasteries and communities of faith in Ireland and England that not only held services but also transformed communities. That was a vision I had for Portland! The specifics of my dream were starting to become clear.

The twist to St. Patrick's churches was that they were hospitality based. He and his people were successful in leading multitudes to Christ by living among them and building relationships with them centered around love and service. The Celtic Christians provided an environment of hospitality that was attractive to local people and the travelers who found lodging in the monastery's rooms. Non-Christians began a relationship with Christ because the Christians they met loved and cared for them. Travelers were able to make a natural transition from unbelief to belief because they received such warm welcomes from communities of faith.[11]

Since I was then similarly working in the "hospitality industry," which in the case of Lincoln Asset Management involved buying, building and managing hotels, I realized with a jolt that here in this book about successful Christians of the past was a model for a new kind of church. It was even deeper than the vision Torre and I had been talking about. It was right in front of me! I realized that Christians can buy hotels as an investment and have the investment fund the mission, but also that hotels had the potential to be an extension of the church's ministry itself. This hospitality ministry could be the most explosive form of evangelism for our century. That helped shape everything.

I began to realize that when a church owns a hotel, it can serve the hospitality needs of travelers better than other hotels because of the church's genuine love for people that is backed by faith. Church attendees can meet on Sundays and Wednesdays in the hotel conference room. In between times, all week long, church members can serve the public in the hotel. They can earn income as paid hotel employees while they fulfill their call to ministry. The hotel income can fund mission work, just like the monasteries of the past that took in paying guests and ran additional businesses on the side to fund their mission.

Hunter's book showed me the advantages of reaching people by serving them. I saw that I had been taught a "Roman" model of church evangelism that was different from Patrick's Celtic model. In church, I would typically present the Christian message and then invite people to decide to believe in Christ and become Christians.[12]

But the Celtic method of evangelism was much more relational. First, you give people a sense of belonging because of your loving welcome and hospitality. You bring them into your community of faith and they feel that they belong. You treat them as friends and talk to them in normal conversations. They pray and worship with you as a natural outgrowth of that relationship. In time, without pressure, these people who didn't have a relationship with Christ until they met you discover in the midst of your friendship that they now believe as you do. Then they make a commitment to Christ.

Hunter used the phrase, "belonging comes before believing."[13] I knew that if what Hunter said were true, a hotel would be a very effective model of evangelism. As soon as a guest walks into the lobby of a hotel and registers for a room, he belongs. A hotel has a new congregation every night.

This dream has been fulfilled today. Because we applied this principle to the hotels owned by Eastside Foursquare Church of Portland, last year we reached tens of thousands of new people without leaving our church grounds!

Consider:

◆ More than 33,000 hotel guests checked in

◆ 42,000 coffee shop customers visited Sacred Grounds Espresso, our on-site coffee shop

◆ Thousands came to neighborhood outreaches sponsored by the hotel

◆ Hundreds used our recovery program, homeless shelter and other ministries

◆ Every day we have opportunities to live out the Gospel before the world through acts of hospitable service because of our business-ministry merger

Developing the dream took time and patience, but it's come about. How about you? Where is your dream at today? Is it strong within you or has it been squelched. If it's been squelched, there is hope. You just need to sort out the phrases you hear from the "Pastor Johns" of the world.

Let me explain:

YOUR FIGHT TO KEEP DREAMING

Early in my ministry, I heard Bill Hybels, pastor of the Willow Creek Community Church near Chicago, say, "Vision leaks." He explained that pastors must keep vision and passion before their members, because it is so easy for them to lose it. People have a hard time following someone else's dream.

My mother had called me a dreamer from the time I was small. She understood that life can be tough and that dreams don't always come true. It might end well in a bedtime story, but that isn't always true in life. She didn't want me to get hurt or to feel the pain of disappointment of a dream gone bad. Like most adults, my mom had discovered that life didn't always turn out the way we thought it should. She wanted to protect me from dreaming too much and becoming disillusioned.

When I was a child, I had dreamed about having enough money to never have to worry about it, as my parents did. I talked about getting a good education and becoming a lawyer, but deep inside I knew I not only wanted to have money. I also wanted to be a pastor. I would often play church, even though we never went to church and I would also play office, even though my parents had never worked in an office. Most of my childhood dreams were only that, but one big dream did come true—the dream of becoming a pastor and going into business.

How about you? What has your dream always been? Is that dream still alive today or has it been crushed?

In the wrong environment, if you dream too much you scare the people around you. That produces opposition. People with big ideas tend to overwhelm others. Most leaders, including the pastors I know, started out as dreamers. When churches and other non-profits are seeking a pastor, they usually look for a visionary. Unfortunately, once the pastor or leader arrives and settles in, he usually meets a few people who want nothing to do with big dreams. They don't want the leader to change anything. They don't understand the importance of creating an environment where big ideas are welcome. Sometimes they don't do it intentionally, but their fears of the unknown stand in the way of progress.

The Bible says that Joseph dreamed of success. In his dreams, he saw his father and brothers bowing down before him and he told them about it. They couldn't forgive him for that.

"'Here comes that dreamer!' they said to each other. 'Come now, let's kill him.'"[14]

When you're a dreamer, you're always rocking the boat. My former denominational supervisors who chose me for my first pastorate in Woodinville were good people, but they didn't have it in their minds that I would make big changes. They didn't even want small changes if it meant they had to depart from their traditions. I had graduated from seminary and was qualified to pastor so they gave

> When you're a dreamer, you're always rocking the boat.

me a church, but the church they chose for me was one step away from shutting down. Then they tried to keep me from being too innovative. But my wife and I believed we could make a difference because we were dreamers.

Outwardly, everything we saw at our first church made the task of merging ministry and business look impossible, but dreamers often see challenge as nothing more than opportunity. We loved the people God gave us and that carried us along, but it was clear that not all people, including some of my fellow pastors, were able to keep their visions alive.

When pastors and other leaders lose their vision, that can affect other leaders as well. During a pastors' conference that my wife and I attended near Washington State's magnificent Mount Rainier, the highest mountain in the Cascades range, I cornered a fellow pastor, whom I'll call Pastor John. He had about ten years more experience in ministry than we did. He had pastored several churches and was now a traveling evangelist.

As I leaned against the trunk of a huge pine tree with that awesome snow-capped mountain in front of us, I told him passionately about our big plans for the church. "We're going to tear down that old building," I said excitedly. "We're going to build a bigger church and reach our neighbors for Jesus. You know, I think I got the church no one wanted, but I don't really care anymore."

Pastor John stood there, expressionless. I just kept talking, my passion tumbling out like an avalanche roaring down the mountainside. "We're going to grow. We've got some new families coming. I want to start . . ."

Pastor John interrupted so coldly that I stopped abruptly. "No way!" he said.

I was completely taken aback. "What?" I asked, incredulously.

"Look, Eric," he said, "I don't mean to be rude, but I give you one-and-a-half, maybe two years, if you're lucky. Then you'll be like all the rest of us. The passion you have is great, but it can't last. You can't sustain that type of passion in ministry. The church will steal it from you."

At first, I couldn't believe what I was hearing. How could a pastor be such a pessimist? I thought our job was to be the visionaries, to lead the charge. Shouldn't a pastor dream big dreams? Or is he just setting himself up for disappointment?

It is easy to become disillusioned in pastoral ministry. Over the next few years, I had to fight the temptation to become like all the other "Pastor Johns" that I met. I realize there can be tough situations in the church and I'm sympathetic to pastors who have been hurt by church politics or hard situations. But not every situation in church work is this way. When these ministers would gather at conferences and meetings, the empty glow of burned-out passion in their eyes revealed a history of disappointment. They had few places where they could share their burdens and few who understood. Declining attendance, low church offerings and offended people deadened their desire to dream. It wasn't as if these leaders were no longer called, but dullness had set up camp in their souls.

Older pastors would get together and count the years to their retirement. They would chat about which RV to buy and how to knock down their payments. They complained about their congregations, not caring whether they reached their community as long as the size of the congregation didn't drop too much on a weekly basis. Conversations ranged from what shoes prevented bunions to the best vacation spots. These pastors had years of education, including seminary study, master's degrees, knowledge of Greek and Hebrew, but they lacked passion—

> Developing vision is not something you can achieve on your own. It is something that God consummates within you.

the ability to feel a dream in the veins of your spirit.

Inside I was screaming, "What about the people? What about the community? What about the dream? Have we forgotten why we do this?!"

The Bible says in Proverbs, "Where there is no vision, the people perish."[15] God literally keeps us alive by birthing vision inside of us. If you keep your sights on Him, you allow Him the opportunity to give you the vision you need to keep from perishing.

Developing vision is not something you can achieve on your own. It is something that God consummates within you. When you devote your life to God, He implants vision directly into your heart. It's a gift, something you couldn't make up on your own. It captures you. Once you have it, you can't possibly do anything else, at least not well. Life tries to squash the vision out of you. It beats you down any way it can. People without a calling keep admonishing you, "Don't rock the boat!"

Allow yourself to receive this dream from God. Don't just pray for a vision, pray for a huge vision! Allow yourself to be open to the most incredible mission-based experience you could think of. And then allow the Lord to do immeasurably more than you could dare ask or imagine.[16] Don't pay any attention to the pessimistic voices inside you that say it can't be done. Dare to dream right now. In the space below, write down the hugest dream you think of, perhaps one that the Lord has been speaking to you about for some time now. If you could do anything, anywhere, at anytime, what would it be?

I dream of

_____

_____

_____

_____

The famous Bible teacher Henrietta Mears (1890-1963) wrote books, spoke all over the world, managed multi-staff ministries, founded publishing companies and conferences centers and directly influenced a generation of college students to go into Christian service including Billy Graham, Bill Bright, Navigators founder Dawson Trotman, Young Life founder Jim Rayburn, seminary president Charles E. Fuller, Bible translator J.B. Philips and US Senate Chaplain Richard Halverson.

On the subject of dreaming big, Dr. Mears wrote:

So many people are willing to be bellhops for the Lord, standing around waiting for someone to give them some little errand to do for Him, instead of asking the Lord to give them His greatest will for their lives. There are so few who want to do the big things for God. You should not be content to pump the organ if God wants you to play on it.[17]

YOU MUST HOLD ONTO YOUR GOD-GIVEN VISION.

It is life itself! Ask God to give you His greatest will for your life. It's easy to "grow-up" and forget your dream, but ask God to remind you. Press on, no matter what! Part of the reason I'm writing this book is to encourage dreamers to keep on dreaming, to latch onto their God-given vision and not let go. To create a sustainable revolution of dreams come true.

God fulfilled my dream of using business enterprises to help an MBE fund the work of the ministry. The same principles you will read about here apply to anyone with a dream. With passion and vision, when God calls you to action, you can change the world. You never know when that call is going to come or where it will take you, but you have to stay open, step through every door of opportunity and keep on dreaming.

YOUR DREAM, TODAY

God always works on the leader first before He works on the dream and that's part of the reason I'm spending so much time in this book to help you lay the proper foundation for becoming an MBE. God is more willing to take risks with us if He sees that we have responded well to His training, died to ourselves and accepted His right to take charge of our lives. He watches us to see if we are fully yielded. If our actions demonstrate that we can be trusted, He gives us big dreams and releases us to bring them to pass.

The risk of liberty is that some people are bound to misuse it. Dream-killers will warn, "Don't turn liberty into license!" I agree that there is always a danger that some people released from their elephant twine will do the wrong thing—the destructive, sinful thing—but that doesn't mean we should keep dreamers bound inside small habitations where they slowly die.

For instance, when teenagers ask to use the car for the first time, tossing them the keys is a risk, but the alternative is not a valid option. No kid ever grew up and became mature without Mom and Dad encouraging them and giving them the freedom to grow. Parents spend years teaching their children through discipline that they can't do things their own way—not so that they can control them for life but so that they can give them the foundation they need to fulfill their destiny.

Children who learn to respect authority and follow the rules of the road are dying to their selfish, independent nature. That's how God often works with us. All of us have a hard time giving up our right to be independent. It's a life work that begins under the discipline of our parents and continues as we grow in God. It is a vital step in the process of fulfilling our dreams.

I encourage you to keep dreaming. Allow God to let your dreams mature. If you've been crushed, allow yourself to dream again. A great future is right around the corner.

SUMMARY

✚ Similar to an ancient technique for training elephants, it's easy to stay tethered to what falsely holds you back. As a leader, you may find yourself falsely tethered to a model of traditional fund-raising. You may be tethered to a false sense of protection and security or by the fear of the unknown.

✚ If God has placed within you a dream, it's okay to be patient. God will invite you to a new sense of liberty when the time is right. Let God develop you before you forcefully tear the twine that binds you and then boldly cross the threshold of your opportunity.

✚ Developing vision is not something you can achieve on your own. It is something that God consummates within you. When you devote your life to God, He implants vision directly into your heart. A dream is a gift, something you couldn't make up on your own. Your dream captures you. Once you have it, you can't possibly do anything else, at least not well.

✚ The pressures of life will try to squash the vision out of you. People without a calling will keep admonishing you, "Don't rock the boat!" But you must hold on to your vision. It is life itself. Like your child-hood dreams of the past, you must "play on" into the night. It's easy to "grow-up" and forget your dreams. But press on, no matter what!

BEGIN YOUR DREAM

Consider for a moment the concept of perseverance. Did you know:

◆ Plato wrote the first sentence of his famous *Republic* nine different ways before he was satisfied.

◆ Cicero practiced speaking before friends every day for thirty years to perfect his elocution.

◆ Noah Webster labored 36 years writing his dictionary, crossing the Atlantic twice to gather material.

◆ Milton rose at 4:00 am every day in order to have enough hours for his *Paradise Lost*.

◆ Gibbon spent 26 years on his *Decline and Fall of the Roman Empire*.

◆ Bryant rewrote one of his poetic masterpieces 99 times before publication and it became a classic.

◆ Thomas Edison performed some 50,000 experiments before he succeeded in producing a storage battery. We might assume the famous inventor would have had some serious doubts along the way. But when asked if he ever became discouraged working so long without results, Edison replied, "Results? Why, I know 50,000 things that won't work."[1]

I offer these examples about perseverance because beginning a dream is seldom an easy task, even if it's what God has called you to do. I encourage you not to run from a difficult location, task or calling. The startup season of a dream is often the hardest part of the process. Weather the startup storms by remembering your vision, what led you to begin the dream in the first place.

This chapter works in conjunction with the following chapter. In both, we'll take a look at some strategies for success as your dream begins to take shape, specifically how choosing the right location for your mission-business venture is extremely vital to beginning work on your dream.

We'll also take a look at some practical tools for counting the personal cost as you begin your dream. When we bought our hotel, we inherited a distressed property and we never imagined what a challenge and stress that would be. Personally, I never examined the high cost to my own health and I'll show you some practical things I did for self-care to sustain my own drive, physically and emotionally.

We'll also show you how you can practically eradicate some of the vision-sappers that inevitably seek to stop the good work you've begun. Part of your job in beginning your dream is to demolish the handiwork of evil so you can provide an anchor for drifting people— we'll show you what that means.

Hang on, you're getting ready to begin your dream and what's coming up is the real guts and glory of the ride.

RUNNING FROM A DREAM

After moving to Portland we began holding meetings for the new church by gathering together a group of like-minded people and holding services. Our church, although very small, had officially begun. Next on the agenda was locating a permanent (or at least semi-permanent) place to begin meeting regularly.

Initially we thought we might plant our church in a city like Canby, Oregon, a smaller, almost rural suburb of Portland. A fellow pastor, Ron Swor from Canby Newlife Foursquare, invited us to start a church somewhere in the area and offered us a variety of resources toward this end. We were very grateful to pastor Ron, but as time went on we began to feel that a small city like Canby wasn't right for us. It began to feel a bit too much like Mayberry—you know, the fictional TV town where nothing moved except dogs on porches rolling over in the sun. We thought instead that we might plant in the Beaverton/Sherwood/Tualatin area of Portland—a hipper, cleaner, safer region more known for up-and-coming professionals. This was certainly our hearts' desire.

Or at least we thought.

As part of our church-planting expedition, I decided to visit a variety of Portland churches so that I could get to know the area. The Beaverton/ Sherwood/ Tualatin area was number one on my list, but for some reason (perhaps just so I could cross off other areas) the first church I visited on a Sunday morning was called New Beginnings. It was located on the northeast side of Portland, a fairly distressed area of the city. From the time my family first arrived in Oregon in January 2002, I had never even considered the possibility of locating our church in the inner city, but here I was. From the moment I walked in the door at New Beginnings, I was in culture shock!

The inner-city neighborhood of northeast Portland was unlike any other place where I had ever been. It just felt old, dank, rained on. New Beginnings's pastor was a former biker. This church was filled with former gang members, drug dealers and addicts, for all I knew. I sat there in my Zanella dress slacks and Ike Behar shirt and I was positive I was in the wrong place.

But during the service, I was in a personal time of prayer and I was shocked to find out that I was actually in the right place, as far as God was concerned. I believe I heard God say to me: "Eric—look around you. This neighborhood. Right here. Forget planting in Beaverton/Sherwood/Tualatin. I am calling you to the inner city of Portland, right in the middle of former gang members, drug dealers and addicts. Plant our new church right here in this blighted area, in the northeast region of the city."

I shook my head. Had I heard right?! Surely God had the wrong guy. I didn't feel adequate for a ministry in that kind of location. Surely God had someone else in mind.

It's funny what you can rationalize the more you don't want to do something. When I truly looked at my own heart, I was sure I had heard God's voice. But like the biblical Jonah, I wanted no part in the pathway God was showing me and I chose to ignore the truth. *I must have heard wrong!*—at least that's what I was telling myself.

> **My insecurity wanted to find safety in what I knew, but God wanted to teach me what I needed to know—His provision.**

So willfully, deliberately, I decided to go the opposite direction. After the service, I ran away to my "Tarshish," which in my case was continuing to plan to plant in the west side of Portland—the Beaverton/Sherwood/Tualatin area. I got as far away as possible from the inner city to find a better place to start a church or so I thought. God said East, but Eric went West.

I know now that I was simply afraid. I was looking at all that I was not. After all, I had a wife and a young daughter and I did not want to raise my family in the inner city. I was looking for the place where all the "nice people live." I wanted it neat. Clean. Comfortable. But God wanted to challenge me to live out my mission as a man who is devoted to Him. My insecurity wanted to find safety in what I knew, but God wanted to teach me what I needed to know—His provision. I had made the commitment years earlier to follow the Lord and it was a commitment "for better or for worse."

Still, I chose to go the other way.

Over in Tarshish, we found a nice, suburban lot where we could build a new home on the west side of Portland, away from the inner city. We put all we had into the place that we were sure God would let us possess and started to put down roots. I found a great new location that would surely work as the center for our newly formed congregation and I decided to submit the plans to my overseers of my denomination.

In order to get permission to plant a new church in West Portland, I needed to meet with the Foursquare denomination's supervisor for that area, a man named Pastor Ron Mehl. (Sadly, at that time he had been diagnosed with chronic lymphocytic leukemia and had only a few months left to live.) Pastor Ron was known and loved in Christian circles as a gentle shepherd, a pastor of pastors. He pastored Beaverton Foursquare Church, which in 1999 had grown to more than 6,000 people, the largest church in Oregon and he had a strong radio ministry on the area radio station. I thought planting a new church in this area would be an easy sell to Pastor Ron. I expected this loving man of God to give me a warm reception when I asked His permission to plant a church in His district.

Imagine my surprise when instead Pastor Ron turned me down cold. He believed the area already had enough churches and he didn't want a hotel/church combination like what I was describing—he was unconvinced this new model would work in such a suburban climate. The only solution, said Pastor Ron, would be if I wanted to plant on the east side of Portland, in a different district. Little did I know that, like Jonah, Pastor Mehl was God's great fish, designed to swallow me up and spit me onshore, headed back in the right direction.

The Foursquare district supervisor over the east side of Portland, Pastor Ted Roberts, who pastored another large church, intimidated me. Even though I had never met him, his reputation as a strong leader had preceded him. Pastor Ted was a former military man. I had just been turned down by a fatherly shepherd and now I had to go to a hard-core military guy.

Reluctantly, I went and amazingly enough he was very receptive. He said he needed more churches in his district and was wide open to thinking outside of the box. I had just been spit up on the shore and God was helping me out through two men in authority who heard His voice. I have come to know Ted as an amazing man who is sensitive to the heart of God. Without his love and firm leadership we would not be where we are today. He has offered great counsel and has stood with us in the line of fire. That day in Ted's office, a door opened before me and I walked right through.

Our plans to plant a church on the east side of town were approved. We started looking for a meeting place, but for quite a while we couldn't find anything. No one would rent to us. Finally, in December 2002 as I was driving down NE Glisan Street I was specifically praying and asking God for a church to rent when I saw a sign that literally said, "Church for Rent." That was the first and last time I have ever seen a sign like that. It might as well have said, "Eric! Here's My location for you! Signed, God." The church was owned by a Russian charismatic group that met on Sundays, so they rented the building to us on Saturday mornings. Our church had the right location to begin meeting regularly. Quickly, we organized our first services and began in the new location.

There's such relief in obeying God's voice. As I walked through the church parking lot on a cold, rainy December morning before our first service in this new location, I reached down and picked up an acorn that I still have today. As I did, I sensed the gentle voice of God saying, "From this acorn I will grow a mighty tree. Eric, remember I own it all."

As I stood up to walk inside the building, I realized that I was on the same street and about a mile and a half away from the New Beginnings Church, the same church where I had run away from God's clear instructions to me a year earlier. God had caught me up and spit me back onto the shore of my calling—the inner city of East Portland. I was back in the right location at last.

DIGGING IN

It's a good thing I had spent so much time in preparing my dream. Before we purchased the hotel property that would become our church's permanent location down the road from our temporary church location on NE Glisan Street, I needed to understand my personal mission and what God was leading me to do. He had to take me back to the right location in East Portland through good mentors, roadblocks and earnest times of prayer.

Then, once I was certain of my assignment, as each new crisis arose I could remind myself and reassure those serving with us that we were standing on a rock of revelation. That knowledge gave us the endurance to conquer personal fears, set goals and break down the barriers that separated us from success.

The spiritual and physical battles that we experienced in those early days of beginning our venture were the most intense of our lives. Some evil force seemed to be at work trying to stop us from completing our project. We were driven to depend on God at a greater level than ever before—and I'll tell you about several of those in this chapter and chapters to come. We had to place our confidence in His power in order to take possession of what He wanted us to have and follow what He wanted us to do. But because of what we had been through, we knew that God brought us to this location. As a result, we were able to hang onto the dream even in the worst times of stress. We were following a purpose much greater than making money. We could not have stood up to those struggles just to earn a living. We had to do it for a cause greater than ourselves in a location that God had chosen.

There was a greater strategy in picking the location we did. We learned it over time. In the hospitality industry, location is a key to financial success. The same is true for a church. We found in the inner city a great location where people were hungry for what we had to offer. They had come to the end of themselves and had nowhere else to turn. When they made a decision to follow Christ, they were dramatically changed. I'm talking total makeover. Our success in people's lives began to dominate our thinking more than the financial pressure. As a result, our situation began to turn around. Their change motivated us to press on.

We learned why the location we picked was so strategic to our mission and this will be key as you study the location for your mission's business venture. Start with the goal of what you want your business to do, then work back from that. For instance, it probably won't work to build a restaurant out in the middle of nowhere without any customers. Or it might not work to set up a thrift store if your ministry is to a Saks Fifth Avenue crowd. Allow prudence, faith and the wisdom of God to lead your decision making. Location is very important. Without the right location, you will not succeed. Here's what we learned, specific to our hotel-church model:

> **Without the right location, you will not succeed.**

1. We located where God wanted us to be

For faith-based mission-business ventures, you'd think this would be a given. But it's easy to run away from a location if that plan seems difficult. The key is to trust God completely. If He is showing you a specific location to minister in by your MBE venture, then rely on His guidance. This is the ultimate key to success. Psalm 127:1 says that unless the Lord builds a place, then the workers labor in vain. God is in control. Inquire of Him and let Him lead you to the right location. Then don't run away.

The emphasis in this first step isn't even so much about the correct location as it is about following God's voice. What does God want you to do? Then do it. No matter how hard or uncomfortable it seems. Let God's guidance initiate your MBE venture.

2. We located in a receptive community

The hotel we found is in a good location because people in the neighborhood needed a church with outreach programs such as drug and alcohol recovery, job training and a family shelter. They also needed a reduction in crime. We brought in the programs and our presence helped facilitate the drop in crime.

Most churches are financially supported by the donations of their members. As urban communities deteriorate, churches often leave the inner cities and relocate to areas where their members feel safer and more comfortable. That means that in order to stay funded, inner-city churches often need to pull away from the areas where they are most needed. The urban core loses the spiritual and practical support that the church could provide.

We operate a business that allows us to stay close to the inner city and fund outreaches to the community without fully depending on donations by those in need. The hospitality model has been a good fit to allow us to accomplish our goals. By operating the hotel and church in this strategic area, we help eliminate crime through the spiritual conversion of criminals into respectable members of society. We pay taxes as a business and also contribute to the city by offering free services that the city would have to fund. We provide classroom space for educational opportunities so that the local population can become successful. Our businesses provides entry-level jobs, training and career advancement. We renovated physical structures to upgrade the neighborhood. We are an asset to the neighborhood and the city, improving the quality of life and restoring a sense of tranquility.

We believe that when our hospitality model for funding community transformation is duplicated by other churches in the future, city officials will try to attract Community-Impact (CI) churches similar to ours to distressed locations just as they currently try to recruit businesses to their enterprise zones.

3. We located where we could flourish in business

Specifically, our location allows us to serve travelers close to Portland International Airport. The hotel we purchased is ideally located on Interstate 205 with two major freeway exits that service the property—Sandy and Killingsworth Boulevards. It is less than two miles from the Portland International Airport. Every day 75,000 cars drive by and can potentially see our sign. We are building a reputation for outstanding customer service and want to become a model for the hospitality industry. Our goal is to represent Christ to our guests—not by preaching but by treating each person who comes through our doors as we would treat Christ Himself.

4. We located in an area that needed transformation

A fourth strategy that came from our location that we had not fully anticipated was the necessity for launching an internal anti-crime campaign to end the illegal activities of the guests who had been frequenting the hotel itself. Most pastors don't envision themselves moving into hell and setting up a church, but that was what we did.

When Eastside Foursquare Church took over management of the former Flamingo Travelodge Hotel in Portland, Oregon, we envisioned a "prosperous" fully functioning hotel serving the public with excellence while the profits helped fund the local projects of our community-impact church. Our operation would exude so much vitality that if we closed our doors, the community would be heartbroken.

However, I know now what the former general manager was thinking when he slyly handed over the hotel keys on June 1, 2004. "Good luck, suckers." He was gone in a flash. You never saw anybody leave town so fast. That should have been our first clue.

People often ask me if I would do it again, knowing what I know now. My answer is probably not. There is a reason God doesn't give you the entire picture when He calls you to your destiny. Don't get me wrong, I love all that is going on now and it has been worth it, but if I had to go back through it all again, it might be more than I could bear.

When we purchased the hotel, we knew it would be a challenge, but we had no idea just how big an undertaking it would be. The owner had not given us a proper opportunity for the needed due diligence in inspecting the property. As a result, once we took over we found severe structural issues that quickly used up all of our reserves.

Everywhere we looked, something had to be fixed, cleaned or in most cases just thrown away. Every day we seemed to find new items in need of replacement. Wires were sticking out everywhere. The entire electrical system was a fire hazard. Plumbing fixtures were stained and broken. Corroded pipes exploded underground or leaked into the walls. The carpets were soiled and moldy. In many places we had to tear down the sheet rock to the bare studs.

The physical plant was not the only issue. Our business plan was based on financial data provided by the owner, who hadn't bothered to tell us that his income came from a rather unusual clientele. Crime was higher in the inner-city neighborhood that bordered the hotel than in many other parts of Portland. After we moved in, we found out why. Many of the small-time criminals operated out of our hotel rooms! Drug dealers, prostitutes and identity thieves rented hotel rooms by the hour or week. Behind the "Do Not Disturb" signs, guests were carrying on illicit businesses. One day we discovered an identity theft ring. Another time we found a drug dealer who had set up his office. Then there was the escort service that conducted business by publishing our hotel phone number. Men would lie in the rooms stark naked with their curtains open waiting for prostitutes to drop in. Yes, unfortunately, the church owned it all. The whole neighborhood knew where to get high on crystal meth except us. We found an abandoned meth lab on the conference center roof. There were so many hypodermic needles on the grounds that some of our youth started a contest to see who could collect the most needles in a day. I think the record was 20.

After a concerted effort by our church, the criminals who had constituted a large share of the business either began attending our services and gave up the life of crime or were driven away. As a result, crime dropped. However, so did hotel income. We no longer had a customer base that could meet income projections. Expenses rose while our income fell almost 50 percent.

(Who says crime doesn't pay?)

YOUR PLAN TODAY

Where will your business-mission set up shop? The location is exceptionally important. It's part of the infrastructure that the Lord will use to facilitate success. My encouragement to you is to spend a solid amount of time thinking and praying through the issue of location. Do this with a trusted team of advisors. Allow the Lord to speak into your life. And if God calls you to Nineveh, resist the temptation to run to Tarshish!

SUMMARY

✛ Begin your dream by doing the hard thing, if that's truly what God has called you to do. Don't run from a difficult location, task or calling.

✛ The startup season of a dream is often the hardest part of the process. Weather the startup storms by remembering your vision; what led you to begin the dream in the first place.

✛ Specifically, the question of where to locate your MBE venture is crucial to answer. At Eastside, we answered that question four ways:

1. We located where God wanted us to be.
2. We located in a receptive community.
3. We located where we could flourish in business.
4. We located in an area that needed transformation.

CHAPTER FIVE

THROUGH THE DARK VALLEY

The young British politician and philanthropist William Wilberforce was discouraged one night in the early 1790s after another defeat in his ten-year battle against the slave trade in England.

Tired and frustrated, he opened his Bible and began to leaf through it. A small piece of paper fell out and fluttered to the floor. It was a letter written by John Wesley shortly before his death.

Wilberforce read it again:

> *"Unless the divine power has raised you up... I see not how you can go through your glorious enterprise in opposing that (abominable practice of slavery), which is the scandal of religion, of England, and of human nature. Unless God has raised you up for this very thing, you will be worn out by the opposition of men and devils.*
>
> *"But if God be for you, who can be against you? Are all of them together stronger than God? Oh, be not weary of well-doing. Go on in the name of God, and in the power of His might."*[1]

Wilberforce took Wesley's letter to heart and pressed on. God was in the work and the work could not be stopped.

There will come a time, shortly after you begin your dream, where you will be tempted to quit. What do you do then? Do you rest in the fact that if God is in your work, then your work cannot be stopped?!

As a pastor, I loved the results of working in people's lives and the way our new church prospered as we threw ourselves into the project together. As a businessman, however, I consistently worried about the bottom line. Our hotel income was so low during the first year-and-a-half that we were having a tough time meeting payments. The financial pressure affected all of us, but as the lead MBE I carried the heaviest responsibility. I knew it was a very real fact that we could lose it all. For several months during that season, the stress would hit me every morning as soon as I woke up and I would very literally run to the bathroom and throw up.

My wife, Rita, as the closest person to me, also felt an incredible weight from this venture. While I was the entrepreneur focused on the finish line, she managed all the little details that had to be accomplished along the way. Rita has an amazing ability to get things done and she felt the stress both as a business woman and my helpmate. She has taught me what a real servant leader looks like. People see me as the upfront visionary, but she is the person behind the scenes making it happen.

The office of our local Foursquare Church district was also under pressure. They had put their reputations on the line for this project. Marc Gale, the assistant district supervisor and Dr. Ted Roberts, the supervisor for our district, had helped me move the project through our denominational process, allowing something to be established that had never been done before. Both men had to field numerous questions from the national headquarters in Los Angeles, using their years of experience and good reputations to back us even when it looked as if it might not work.

Looking back, I believe that God blinded us to things we should have seen before we bought the hotel. If we saw what we were getting into, we would never have made the move. Most people would have walked away from the deal. Apparently our dream of a great tomorrow had caused us to advance naively into enemy territory when most people would have retreated. I have been asked many times,

"How could you have missed this?" There was no great strategy here, it's because we were simply ignorant of the danger that awaited us. Hopefully, you can learn from our mistakes.

The specifics of the path that the Lord leads you down will undoubtedly look different, but the temptation to quit will undoubtedly come. So what do you do? When the pressure to pack up and go home hits you strongly, how do you survive?

TURNING A CORNER

When God backs a venture that doesn't readily make sense from a human point of view, sometimes it is His way of keeping you humble and continuing the process of your spiritual growth. If merging a hotel and a church had been easy, I might have been tempted to take the credit. But the financial shortfall that soon awaited us after beginning the venture took me to an entirely new level of embarrassment, stress and total dependence on God. By cleaning up our clientele (i.e. the drug and prostitution business), we inadvertently

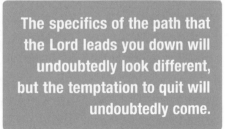

The specifics of the path that the Lord leads you down will undoubtedly look different, but the temptation to quit will undoubtedly come.

drove away our "best" cash-paying customers. When the books were tallied, we were short $1.5 million dollars to finish our remodel. That's not the type of liability you can slap down a credit card for and erase any time soon. We were in serious trouble.

My strategy simply became to keep going. I didn't know what else to do. This was not a good time to boast and start giving tours to other churches to show them our exciting new "business venture" and our "community-impact church." In fact, we didn't even put up a sign with our church name on it. There were no press releases or banners announcing "Under New Ownership." If this thing failed—and it was looking like it was going to—we wanted to keep this as quiet as possible.

Tours would have helped raised support, at least prayerfully if not financially, but there were other embarrassing reasons we felt we couldn't hold tours for local ministers. A few days after we arrived, one of our pastors was walking through the parking lot when a garish woman slinked up to him and said, "Hey there, big boy! I've got a couple of hours. Want to go party?" If someone didn't understand the vision of what we were undertaking, we never would have heard the end of that.

People looked to me to speak resurrection life into this dead place. After all, I was the MBE who had driven the project through. Many people had sacrificed because they believed in the dream, but I was overwhelmed. Why didn't we go plant in the safe suburbs? One day a drunk walked out of his second-floor hotel room and peed off the balcony. One of our staff members said to me ruefully: "Now we know for sure that this ain't Canby!" Boy, did he get that one right!

Fortunately, change was right around the corner. John 1 (the Message) mentions that whenever Jesus moves into a neighborhood, things change for the better. The Bible calls the change "glory." A paraphrase of this passage might read: "The Word became flesh and blood and moved into the neighborhood. We saw the glory with our own eyes."[2] The same thing happened when the people of God moved into this dilapidated neighborhood. We were carrying the glory of God.

Our aim became to run this hotel with a moral and sound business framework. That meant we needed to clean it up and attract business and family clientele from the nearby Portland airport. Once that happened, money would start flowing again, we'd get out of debt and we could fund various programs that would help the surrounding neighborhoods. We certainly weren't going to continue funding our hotel by bringing in the drug and prostitution business. But for the change to happen, we needed to usher in a shift in how our "regulars" viewed our hotel. We were willing to help them, sure, but for many of them, simply, it would mean that they needed to leave.

One of our first specific challenges was getting rid of an on-site bar. Now, there are plenty of people who enjoy a casual drink with dinner or what have you and my purpose in this chapter is not to offer a full-blown treaty for or against alcohol. The problem with this particular bar was that it had nothing to do with being a friendly neighborhood place "where everyone knows your name," and it had everything to do with perpetuating harm and destruction in our neighborhood. It's tough to fully convey how a bar such as this had such a negative community impact on a neighborhood like ours, in the inner city. Alcohol was a major problem for many families and individuals in this area and the alcohol fueled a variety of other problems such as fighting, noise and lewd behavior including a clientele that favored prostitution, drugs and violence. Simply put, this bar needed to go.

Here was the challenge. The bar was on our property. We owned the lease. How's that for a moral quandary—our church was making money from a bar that perpetuated evil. Wanting the bar gone as a church was a simple matter. But as a business and legal entity, it was much more difficult. Our church was put in the place of honoring a 20-year lease for a bar and restaurant on the property that came with our purchase. We were polite to the owner and we explained our position to him several times. We offered a variety of solutions and explained our need to help end drug use and prostitution within the neighborhood. He could see that we weren't particularly pleased to have him there. Yet he was determined to stick to his rights and we couldn't see any legal means to remove him.

So we went to a higher source. We enlisted the help of the Oregon Liquor Control Commission, the agency that strictly enforces laws pertaining to alcohol sales. They sent in undercover agents. Several Portland police officers would park their patrol cars in front of the bar right before closing. Patrons who had too much to drink could not simply get in their cars and drive away like they used to do, nor would we rent them a room.

And we went to the ultimate Higher Source. We prayed.

Finally, after many discussions with the owner, he found his price, communicated it to us and we bought out his lease. It wasn't a very happy parting. In fact, during one point in the transaction he said, "Your pastor is possessed!"

He was right about that. God's presence lives inside of His children—that's for sure.

The closing didn't happen smoothly, either. But good things would eventually come from it. The bar was scheduled to close in the middle of August. On the last night the bar was open, bar management threw a huge party. Pastor David Walmer (Eastside Church's executive pastor and the general manager of the hotel) and I worked the front desk that night. We knew what went on in there and we wanted to be on hand in case things got rough (you have to realize the entry door to the bar faced our hotel—they were about 20 feet away from each other). We could hear patrons shouting obscenities. Bikers making as much noise as possible. We watched people stumble out of the bar so drunk they could barely walk.

Fortunately, the Lord can redeem any situation. That night a young man I'll call Bob stumbled out of the bar and crossed the driveway to the hotel front office where David and I were working. As he entered the lobby, he asked drunkenly, "What time is it? They just kicked me out of there!" He had blond hair, was fairly tall and fine featured, but obviously had experienced a rough life.

True to our mission, I greeted him like a friend, then asked, "Why did they kick you out?"

"Because I got too fresh with a girl," he said.

I was thinking this guy had to be pretty bad to get kicked out of that bar, considering what I know goes on there every night. "So, where do you live?" I asked.

He told me he lived up the street a few blocks away, so, seeing he was in no position to drive, I offered to give him a ride home. We got in the car and drove six blocks to the place where he lived. On the way he said, "I need a job. Would you hire me?" He did not have a clue who I was because I had not told him. He thought I was just a friendly hotel manager. As we stopped in front of his house, I decided to be more direct. I said, "You probably need more than a job."

"My life is a mess," he admitted. He talked on and on. I had never heard so much swearing in one conversation.

Finally I suggested, "Why don't you come back to the hotel tomorrow at 10 a.m? We can talk more then."

The next morning, I wasn't sure if he would show up and I was tired from overseeing the bar closing, but I still made sure that I was at the hotel and in my office by 10 a.m. He actually came by and talked some more. He thought it was a job interview. I didn't tell him I had no intention of hiring him in that condition. I asked him some questions about his work experience. After more conversation, he took a new turn. He said, "I don't know if you're religious, but I don't think God likes me much anymore. In fact, I think He's forgotten me." He was cussing the whole time. When he paused I said, "I'm not into religion. I'm into relationship. God doesn't hate you, nor has He forgotten you. In fact, God loves you so much that He kicked you out of the bar and into the church. Bob, this is not a hotel. This is the church."

"Huh?" he said.

"The church bought this hotel in June and I am the senior pastor. None of this is a hotel. It's really all a church."

He couldn't fathom that this was a church. Bob was so shocked that his words started flooding out. He would curse with one sentence and ask me to forgive him for cursing with the next. After five minutes of this stream of sentences he stopped and looked at me. I saw a hardened addict who had lived a tough life, now with a tear rolling down his cheek saying, "So how do I get this relationship with Jesus you're talking about anyway?"

Together we knelt down in my office. It was a radical conversion, one of the most amazing I have ever seen. He didn't know how to pray so I said, "I'll help you. Just say that you are sorry for the things you did." He prayed without stopping. He was so broken up that it took him about ten minutes just to confess everything he had done in the past 24 hours, let alone his whole life. He had a lot to confess!

When he finished, we went outside onto the hotel campus. I saw several of our staff members and introduced him. "This is Bob. He just said yes to a relationship with Christ." Everyone could tell that this was someone who had experienced God. They were excited and warmly welcomed him into our family.

Bob sounded kind of dazed when he said, "I feel like a new person. Something has changed inside of me. This is weird. It's the weirdest I've ever felt. I feel like a weight has been lifted off of me and that I'm somehow new."

His eyes cleared. His face cleared. The glory of God was visible on him. It was a massive transformation. I asked him, "You said that you want work? Since you've done construction, I have some demolition work to be done. The bar closed last night and now we're going to destroy it. You know how to work a hammer?"

DEMOLISHING THE HANDIWORK OF EVIL

The next morning Bob began on our construction crew. He stayed on the job for several months and almost single-handedly tore out the bar and threw its old pieces of evil in the dumpster, just as Lazarus stood up in the grave and walked out—not only leaving death behind but also destroying the tomb.

A half a year after closing the bar, the Portland police stopped by and told us that we had already done more in six months than the police had been able to do in ten years. Through the efforts of our pastors, church members and staff working with the local police, the efforts of our community-impact church had caused a dramatic decline in crimes in the neighborhood. The police showed us statistics that documented the fact. Crimes such as rape, homicide, robbery, aggravated assault, burglary and theft were now lower than a third of what they had been in the community before we arrived. Calls for service to the police dropped so significantly that the police commended us for accomplishing what they had been unable to do without us.

Our hotel soon became one of the safest ones in Portland. Six months after closing the bar, the old dive that had been destroying the neighborhood had become transformed into a beautifully carpeted church where people could find love and meet God. When we had a Christmas party for our staff, Bob was there to help put up the tree and celebrate with us.

Bob was the first person to accept Christ through our hotel ministry. His life was our first resurrection. His conversion of the bar was the lasting evidence that Jesus has triumphed over the grave—not only for Bob but also for the tens of thousands of people whose lives we have touched just in the first few years of this venture.

In January 2005, our church made the move from the Russian church location that we had been renting to the hotel's campus. For the first few months we met in the former bar that was now a meeting room. Later, when we moved the church services upstairs to a larger location in the conference center, we converted this former bar into a children's center and youth concert venue called the Haven. Where minors once were not allowed, they now are welcomed and loved.

For some time after that, people would come looking for the bar. When they found out it was now a children's church, they were shocked. They simply couldn't believe it.

When we established Eastside Foursquare Church at this location, we set out to meet people's needs better than a bar or anything else could. We did not have a dark side like the bar. We knew how to bring light and be a blessing. We wanted to be a stable influence that could change an entire community. When I was still in Washington State, I received some wise advice from Dr. Joseph Fuiten, senior pastor of Cedar Park Assembly of God in Bothell, Washington. He stressed the value of maintaining a physical church building to give stability to members and a visible place of refuge for the community. The physical building that we bought for our hotel and community-impact church was a wreck when we started, but with prayer and a lot of hard work, we transformed it into a new community icon. Over the years since we moved in, we have given our community a place of light, love, stability and people they can count on.

The world is constantly drifting. Even though people think they want to be self-sufficient, when a crisis comes they realize they need a church as an anchor in their lives. They need to know that we are there for them and that the church will continue to exist. Dr. Fuiten told me, "Pastor the people God gives you and not the people you wish God would give you." Some people with needs come and go. They use up our resources and move on, but we are here for them, too. We have made a commitment to stay for the sake of the people God has given us.

Eastside Foursquare Church is not moving away. We have set down our stakes. When we changed our corner of the inner city into

> When we were tempted to give up, we had to remind ourselves that we aren't running a sprint, but a marathon.

a new business and family-friendly model, we began to attract new clientele. We even received from our denomination the additional $1.5 million we needed to complete the renovation. And I stopped throwing up every morning. Today things have turned around. We don't intend to leave.

When we moved into the community, we knew the process would take a long time. When we were tempted to give up, we had to remind ourselves that we aren't running a sprint, but a marathon. Our success would not be overnight, but it would last. Most importantly, we needed to realize that if God was in our work, then our work could not fail. God was leading this enterprise. Our invitation was to work hard, yes, but ultimately to rest in Him. He would not disappoint.

A CASE FOR COMMUNITY IMPACT CHURCHES

I'm writing this book for leaders from a variety of non-profit organizations. That's truly a passion of mine—I want to help teach you to fund your mission in a sustainable way. Additionally, I have a specific passion and heart to help develop more community impact churches such as ours. Let me explain why I feel that way.

As of the writing of this book, about 1,000 people call Eastside home. We're actually an umbrella church today and have four different English-speaking and two Spanish services at our main campus. We also have several off-site locations throughout our community and we've established another campus in a differ-

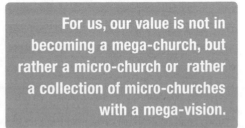

For us, our value is not in becoming a mega-church, but rather a micro-church or rather a collection of micro-churches with a mega-vision.

ent country. By today's mega-church standards, we aren't huge. But I believe we're doing exactly what we need to be doing.

People often judge the success of a congregation by its size rather than the changed lives of the people who attend. Even a pastor can fall into the trap of using attendance numbers to validate his ministry. I explain to people that Eastside is here to stay, whether large numbers of people attend or not.

Our value as a ministry and our community impact aren't measured by how many seats we fill at our weekend services, even though there is nothing wrong with a growing church and it can be a significant sign of health. For us, our value is not in becoming a mega-church, but rather a micro-church or rather a collection of micro-churches. with a mega-vision. In other words, we see ourselves as part of a global movement of transformation—one person and one community at a time. Each person's life has value and can have a positive impact on others around him.

It might sound like one of our goals is not to increase our size. That's not true. We are heading in the direction of having multiple branch locations all across our city. As a church we want to win as many people to the Savior as possible. We want as many people as possible to have healthy homes and families, to be free from chaos and addictions and to live lives of victory, strength and confidence. We want to possess, acquire and build as much as we can for the sake of our mission. We hope to continually transform more communities and eventually our whole city, region and state. But we want to do this with sincerity and authenticity. Our goal isn't to get large numbers simply for the sake of getting large numbers. Transformed hearts and lives are always of utmost importance.

One of the young women who came to Eastside as a drug abuser and prostitute now brings a whole row of new people to church each week, many from her former life. That's the kind of church growth I love.

It's easy today for people to grow up without the moral underpinnings instilled by parents. People crave something more, so they explore the supernatural realm, but without a biblical framework to guide them, they look in the wrong places to find God; they trust their feelings more than the words of Scripture. Stable community-impact churches are there for them when they recognize they need someone trustworthy and committed who has the wisdom and experience to show them a way out.

Some churches establish a peaceful coexistence with evil. People drive into town on Sunday by the thousands and then drive out while the streets around the church remain the same. Community impact churches are not defined by those who attend on Sunday but by their passion for love and justice on weekdays in the neighborhood. They don't expect non-Christians to solve all the social problems.

Our on-site recovery program, Freedom House, has restored the lives of young men and reunited them with their families. We support a job training program and a brand new homeless shelter. We have taken on the assignment of meeting head-on the physical day-to-day needs of the poor and those who can't help themselves. We provide places of hospitality where people can come just as they are. We do whatever it takes to reach them with God's love.

A verse in the Bible says, "Do not love the world or anything in the world. If anyone loves the world, the love of the father is not in him."[3] This verse carries an important message to explain to Christians that they should live a life that is pure and above reproach. The church, however, has sometimes used this message to avoid people in the world because of fear of contamination. The unfortunate result has been a nearly complete separation between congregation and community, with the church property as the boundary line.

We might as well admit it: Our love-in-action has not been strong enough to overcome our fear of people who don't come to us in traditional ways, meet our terms and participate in church as we have known it. Even though we are imperfect ourselves, we're scared of people outside the church who have empty eyes and unfulfilled lives. They don't look like church people. They don't act like us. They don't dress like us. That's because they need our love.

In order to love the people of the world, we have to get to know them relationally first. Then we can show them our God.

Part of our plan to remedy that was to make friends with our community. We decided to have an open house and invite everybody in. We realized that many people in our community would not come to church every week, but some of them would come on a holiday like Easter. We decided to set a target date of Easter Sunday 2005 for our first public service in the new building.

First the bar was converted to a Haven and then the second-floor meeting room was converted to a sanctuary. Nine months from the time we took possession of the hotel property, we gave birth to our first public service. We sent out 20,000 mailers to the local community inviting people to church on Easter. On the surface, you would not think that our small church of 60 or 70 people at that time could have an impact on one city block, let alone a city of half a million, but we didn't look at what we lacked. We looked at what we could become if we depended on God to help us reach the people.

By the Saturday night before Easter, we still had not finished carpeting the stairs to the second-floor meeting room but everyone pitched in and we made the deadline. From the despair of the summer before, we had resurrected our dream. We had made the dream a reality. Every church experiences a swell in attendance on Easter, but we nearly tripled in one day. Many stayed and we have never looked back. Travelers at the hotel just passing through and people from the community with transient needs are welcomed along with our regular members who love to serve others.

That first Easter Sunday, people came because they received a mailer. Now they come because of the amazing people of Eastside and our community impact on the city. Maybe they need help or they want to help somebody else, but either way they believe our church is just the right place for them. I believe that our church and hotel model is one of the most important community projects in Portland right now. It's giving people hope and a future. What other cities call urban renewal we call resurrection life.

Every time our neighbors pass by, they see something new at our hotel and church. New signs. New landscaping. A coffee shop. Fresh paint. Old run-down rooms that had been badly trashed converted into one of Portland's finest hotels. Lives restored and resurrected in an environment of hope and love.

"Jesus said to her, 'I am the resurrection and the life. He who believes in Me will live, even though he dies; and whoever lives and believes in Me will never die.' . . . Jesus called in a loud voice, 'Lazarus, come out!' The dead man came out, his hands and feet wrapped with strips of linen and a cloth around his face. Jesus said to them, 'Take off the grave clothes and let him go.'"[4]

Is God calling you to launch a community-impact ministry? Maybe you have been running from that call, as I did or maybe you have been running toward it. If your specific call is to launch or help launch a community-impact church, here are important lessons we learned along the way. Keep these in mind as you move forward.

1. Clearly define your vision

When we felt that we were going to lose everything, we were able to persist because we knew what we were called to do. Before you start, write the vision just as God told the prophet Habakkuk,[5] then define your mission statement based on prayer and the needs that you see in your community. Your statement should include the answers to these questions:

For what purpose do you exist?

Who will you reach? Who will you not reach?

How do you want your community to be different?

What role do you want your organization to play in your community?

What will success look like?

Create a specific, workable plan to carry out your vision based on prayer, the Scriptures and an honest analysis of yourself, your church, your community and your available resources. Use the services of experts in the field.

2. Communicate your vision frequently

Communicate your vision to your organization members, family, congregation and business associates. As they understand it, they will embrace it and you can follow the mission together. You may want to gather a team and define short-term goals that will build some immediate momentum as well as define some long-term goals that will give you a ministry that lasts.

You will need to communicate your vision more than once. Have regular meetings where you reiterate what's going on to your staff and supporters. Have the vision statement in strategic places where you and your team will be reminded of it.

Don't be afraid to launch a big vision. If God gives it to you, He will help you accomplish it if you are willing to pay the price.

Continue to communicate your vision as people need to see and understand your vision clearly so they can own it and help implement it.

3.Build unity to accomplish the vision together

One of the regulars who used to shoot drugs at the Flamingo Travelodge before we bought the hotel told us what it used to be like in the old days. Jeff still remembers the hotel room number where some of the drug dealing took place because he went there so often. He said that no "normal" people ever stayed at the hotel unless they were old folks who still remembered it from past glory days when it was the Best Western Flamingo, the classiest place in town.

Jeff had an extensive criminal record with five major felonies and no way to get a job. After he found a relationship with Christ and changed his life through his association with our church, we recognized his potential and gave him a job on the night shift at the front desk. Because of our relationship and his desire to build up the hotel business with us, he was willing to take on the criminals who still tried to check in. He could recognize them from the old days. When they tried to get a room, he had the courage to tell them they were no longer welcome.

Everyone learned to recognize the signs of illicit activity and notify our GM and Jeff—the smell of marijuana coming through the door, the look of people getting ready to party. Sometimes criminals would still slip in and rent a room on another shift and Jeff, David or I would have to go to their rooms and ask them to leave.

Jeff is tall and his presence can be intimidating. Few people wanted to mess with him. Even when people yelled at him, he always stood his ground. Today he has graduated from college and is doing well in his walk with God.

At Eastside, people don't just go to church services together. We do the work of hospitality together every day. To help build and own vision together, we've gone to more informal settings together. We've worked at listening to our leadership and giving each person an empowered voice. We've allowed them to express their understanding of the vision and suggest their role within it. And we've affirmed them by giving them responsibilities in areas where they excel and encourage others to follow their lead.

4.Make a long-term commitment to the vision

True and lasting change seldom happens overnight. After about four years of perseverance, we had remodeled almost every guest room in the hotel and our outreach ministries were running well. The vision continued to unfold before us in greater ways than we had ever dreamed possible. We made it because we had a long-term commitment to see this through.

Have you done the same? Make a commitment not to give up when the going gets tough. Keep working until the mission is a reality. Dream great dreams but be willing to slow down, stop or change direction if you are going the wrong way.

NEW ADVENTURES WITH GOD

God may be calling you to begin a community-impact church. Everything we have done at Eastside can be duplicated. In fact, duplication has become the next dream that drives us. In Chapter 10 and the Appendix you will find more information on how our Christian Asset Network (CAN) assists pastors and leaders to begin hotel ownership themselves.

Torre Morgal and I partnered to form CAN in order to help churches and ministries bridge the gap between ministry and the hospitality business. Through CAN, we can help a church locate a hotel

> Through CAN, we can help a church locate a hotel property, finance it, meet hospitality industry standards and manage a hotel like ours, from start to finish.

property, finance it, meet hospitality industry standards and manage a hotel like ours, from start to finish.

If you are the leader of a church or ministry and decide to launch out into the deep waters of the hotel industry, some people will tell you that it is impossible. Maybe they're right. It is impossible if you are just one person. But if you have a partnership with CAN, you are no longer alone. You have a force behind you—people who know the market and have developed strategic partnerships that can make it work. That places you on a level playing field where anything is possible.

And then there is the power of God. With Him, nothing is impossible. In fact, I wouldn't recommend even thinking about owning a hotel unless you consult Him first. As you open for business, you will meet the public and be confronted with situations you never imagined before. Your "church" will be open not 5 or 6 or even 20 hours a week but 24 hours a day, 7 days a week. If you love bringing people into the Kingdom of God, you'll love the opportunity, but if you want a life of ease it's not for you.

You may not end up in the inner city as we did, but you will meet people like those I describe in the next chapter whose bizarre behavior causes you to pause, laugh and even wonder how you got yourself into this situation in the first place.

If you're open to new adventures, I invite you to turn the page.

SUMMARY

✦ Shortly after you begin your dream, expect a season to come where you want to quit. That's a normal part of the MBE process. Your venture would not be worth doing if it was easy or without personal cost.

✦ A simple strategy in this season is the most straightforward one: keep going. Don't make this a season where you quit, complain or showcase your MBE venture yet, simply keep your hand to the plow, figure out what needs to be done and keep doing what you've been called to do.

✦ You will undoubtedly face moral quandaries as part of your difficult season—times and experiences where you will suffer from doing the right thing.

Do the right thing, even when it's painful. A huge part of your calling on the way to community transformation is to eradicate evil, the things that hurt people's lives.

✦ As your MBE venture weathers this initial season, keep your focus on your vision. You will begin to impact your community in positive ways. Make sure that you:

1. Clearly define your vision.
2. Communicate your vision frequently.
3. Build unity by accomplishing the vision together.
4. Take a long-term commitment to the vision.

CHAPTER SIX

IMMERSE YOURSELF IN THE DREAM'S REALITIES

"She's trying to kill him!"

We had only been in the hotel three months, but already the novelty had worn off this kind of exclamation. The man shouting this had rushed into the lobby, so I followed him to the parking lot to see what was going on. Sure enough, there was a large, irate woman cursing and throwing rocks like missiles at a little guy dodging them on the second floor walkway. It was almost funny. I'm not sure if I was more worried about him or the windows. Someone called the police.

What is it like trying to run a business on faith-based terms? Becoming an MBE means you and your team will be called upon to respond to a variety of situations with Christ-like grace. In the early days, nothing that happened at the hotel surprised us. We needed to call the police for some new incident every two or three days. Even when we didn't, they would come by and ask to see our guest registrations. Whenever they found someone wanted by the law, they would go to the room and arrest them. For a while the Portland Police Department could count on multiple arrests at our place every week. They were a big help in cleaning up nests of corruption and making our faith-based business one of the safest places in town.

This time when the policeman arrived we were able to resolve the rock-throwing incident. However, just as he was getting ready to leave, a housekeeper walked up to us, motioning toward a room saying, "Come, you've got to see this." The officer and I followed her to one of the rooms she had been cleaning. Inside was a pile of passports, drivers' licenses and blank checks. Someone had been operating an identity theft ring on our property and we didn't even know it.

Later, as I walked with the officer to his patrol car, he said, grinning humorously, "I heard a rumor that a church bought this place." (We hadn't yet placed any signs on the property to identify ourselves as a church or a church-owned business.)

"That's not a rumor," I said cheerfully. "It's true."

He laughed and said, "What church would be that stupid? Don't they know that this is the biggest crack house in Portland?" Approaching his patrol car he turned, reached out with a warm handshake and asked, "So, what do you do here?"

I paused for a moment, not sure how to respond, then said, "I guess you could say that I'm the senior pastor of the biggest crack house in Portland."

He burst out laughing. He just couldn't believe it. When we both stopped laughing he said something I will always remember. I think about it even today if I ever start wondering what in the world I am doing here. The policeman said with emotion, "I don't go to church. I'm not religious, but I always thought that if a church could be involved in a community, this is what they should be doing. Way to go, pastor. You've got a lot of guts."

That dynamic is what we want to talk about in this chapter. Think of today's Christ-centered MBE ventures as modern mission outposts, places that help, encourage, refresh and train people to lead new lives. In the case of our hotel, we found something that was broken and were eventually able to transform it into something beautiful—an oasis in the desert where we are working and doing life together. People receive the water of life at Eastside and the hotel and it keeps on springing forth day after day because it comes from Jesus, the foundation of our faith.

The following are some of the lessons we have learned that have allowed us to succeed, both as a mission and as a business, to ultimately operate on a daily basis with the goal of meeting the needs of the world by love. Your MBE venture can do the same.

A PROSPERING MISSION

It does take "a lot of guts" to believe that the unstoppable power of God operating through a faith-based business like a hotel can transform communities and point people to Christ. Although American preachers have been under attack all the way to the U.S. Senate for preaching a "prosperity" Gospel, the Bible never said that God didn't want the Church to prosper—within the proper definitions of the Word. God only chastised Israel when they misused their prosperity. When the Church truly prospers, it's a sign of God's blessing, not a reason to launch a Congressional investigation. In fact, if senators knew their Bibles in passages like Deuteronomy 28, they would investigate churches when they stopped prospering! That is a biblical sign that believers are in sin. Our prosperity provided the funding we needed to take over "the biggest crack house in Portland" and make it a place of refuge. We define prosperity as operating our business with integrity, making a profit, then reinvesting that profit in the community for good.

Historically, there are many examples of prospering missions. Beginning in the first century, the Church ran faith-based businesses. Mission and money came together so that the Church could accomplish the purposes of God and pay for it with wealth generated by private enterprise. Pastors, deacons and laymen started income-producing companies with solid business practices that paid for the church's outreach missions. People still gave offerings, but the missions weren't dependent on them. In the book of Acts, people donated real estate for the work of the Church, which was a social mission based on helping people in need. The driving force was Jesus.

If you ever saw the 1963 movie *Lilies of the Field*, where actor Sidney Poitier became the first black man to win an Academy Award for Best Actor, you may remember that it was his task to come up with building materials for German nuns who wanted to build a chapel at an Arizona mission. He had to use whatever materials he could find in the local area. The ladies worked hard planting crops and milking their single cow.

Long before that, in the Spanish missions of California, missionaries planted crops to feed themselves and others in the local community. Their kitchens and bakeries served hundreds of meals a day. They raised livestock for wool, leather and tallow and bred horses to plow the land. They started schools to teach Native Americans how to function in industrial and agricultural environments and to become self-sufficient, regardless of the availability of game.

Most people don't realize that the famous fruit we enjoy today from California orchards was not indigenous to that region. The only fruits explorers found there were berries. Diligent Spanish missionaries brought fruit seeds from Europe and planted orange, grape, apple, peach, pear and fig seeds. Those people were fruitful in a multitude of ways. They did not found mission churches with the expectation that they would be supported entirely by the local people. Their goal was self-sufficiency for themselves and the local community. They built stone aqueducts and formed baked clay pipes to carry water over many miles to the mission. They used sand and charcoal to purify it for drinking and also used the water to turn grinding wheels and other machinery. Sometimes the missions provided for the military forces at a nearby fort. At San Juan Capistrano, they built the first foundry and forged tools, nails, gates, hinges and even cannons for the forts.

> In every faith-based business, the mission is more important than the money.

In every faith-based business, the mission is more important than the money. The word "mission" comes from the Latin word *missum,* which means sent, or *missionem,* which means the *act of sending.* We derive the word "apostle" from the Greek equivalent of the word for mission. Apostles and missionaries are messengers of a new life, but it takes money to carry the message and establish credibility as the people of God. As you may recall from the example of St. Patrick, historically mission outposts existed not only for evangelism and religious instruction but also as early hotels for travelers who needed a place of peace and safety. Our hotel follows a similar trend. It's a refuge for business and leisure travelers; they receive a filling from us and it keeps on springing forth day after day because it is a filling from Jesus. He said this: "Indeed, the water I give him will become in him a spring of water welling up to eternal life."[1]

Our hotel is an expression of who we are as Christians. It is a symbol of something we believe in. We provide hospitality through a faith-based business that ministers to travelers and also provides a self-sustaining source of funding for our work. As MBEs, we embarked on a mission to help people in a spiritual desert to find water. We opened a place of business and installed a self-sustaining pump called a hotel that produces water to restore life to this community.

If I were a missionary in a land dried up by famine, I would understand that my first task had to be finding the local residents a fresh source of water. Maybe I would discover that someone before me had installed a pump, but over time it had become rusty and quit working. I might have to make repairs, replace the engine and kick it a couple of times, but after hard work and a few false starts, water would begin to flow. In the arid wasteland of the human condition, people are not always ready to receive the living water of Christ, but if they have a natural thirst they will always receive someone who offers water.

A severely dehydrated person is weak, dizzy and confused. A spiritually dehydrated person is the same. As a Church, we can't be satisfied with pumps that produce only a trickle of water once a week. We must repair the pumps so that water flows night and day. At Eastside, our solution was to open a hotel. Jesus is the only Oasis who can save people from the spiritual desert in the world. Presenting Him as an option requires a sustainable funding model that provides an enduring wellspring of life. The integration of business and ministry—a faith-based business—allows us to do that.

Some American churches that want to operate centers for urban missions lack a means of self-sustaining funding. They must continually raise offerings and solicit donations. They may lose income when members move to the safer suburbs. In some of those instances, faith-based business entities that create profits could be a solution to help fund this valuable work. Businesses could provide jobs for people in the church and the local community and offer not only training but also discipleship experiences under mature Christian leaders.

THE SPECIFICS OF SUCCESS

At Eastside, we operate a merger of church and business. The church is a for-profit hotel but we never forget that we are a church that never closes its doors. Some people have literally told us, "If you had not been here, I'd be dead."

Sometimes individuals check in to a hotel when their lives are at the lowest point, contemplating suicide. At our hotel they find people who care. Guests sense the godly atmosphere and feel comfortable talking about personal needs. Every year people give their lives to Christ after coming to the hotel, the church and the outreach ministries. Those are the rewards that we live for.

Here are seven lessons we have learned that have allowed us to succeed at both our mission and our business.

1. We respect our paying guests

A faith-based business always functions on at least two levels. You must be sensitive to the needs of the poor and homeless or other people you are called to help, but you must also remain conscious of the needs of your customers—in our case, our paying guests.

Successful faith-based businesses value people before profits, but that doesn't mean that you can neglect proper business practices. Operating a business with integrity and excellence means meeting the needs of your customers so that they receive full value for their dollar. That is one of the ways you insure that the funding stream for missions that comes from your business won't dry up.

When we first opened the hotel, we envisioned a place where we could not only operate a hospitality business with excellence but also where we could carry out social service work. Early on, however, we received wise counsel from Glenn Burris, Jr., general supervisor for the Foursquare Denomination, who suggested that we not use the hotel as a homeless shelter or the campus as a place for social service.

While it might have been right to house the homeless here if we were just a traditional church, as a hotel we had to make the right connection with travelers. We had to honor their needs and serve them in the best way possible or we would not be meeting the standard of God. We would not be able to receive the income that we needed to support our other ministries.

As much as I learned to love the homeless, we had to make the decision that most of the time a hotel cannot function as a homeless shelter while it is providing hospitality to paying guests. Even though we might have extra rooms available, we are a hotel that has to earn the patronage of customers who require certain standards in their environment. We decided that we would not be able to maintain our hotel clientele if we provided lodging for homeless people who had not only been living in the streets but also had other physical and mental problems, including strange or threatening behavior.

Sometimes it was hard for other churches and businesses to understand our position. We still take a lot of criticism to this day from Christians who figure that because we have a hotel we have spare rooms and therefore need to take in any homeless person who shows up. People have scornfully said to us things such as, "And you call yourself a church?" Ironically, business owners often understand this tension better than other Christians.

For some time at the beginning, churches would do "drive-by drop-offs"—bringing a homeless person to our door and dropping him off and driving away. Then they would criticize us if we didn't keep him there. We solved that by supporting a professionally staffed family shelter with outstanding lodging that has resulted in changed lives. More about that later.

2. We have a unique product and offer consistent outstanding service

Every business needs to find a need and fill it. Once you understand your capabilities and relate them to a perceived need of the population, you can establish yourself in the right niche market. You find out how to satisfy a targeted group of consumers in a creative way. Every business has competition, so you know from the outset that the way you carry out your business will be even more important in defining you as a superior option than what you sell your customers.

We are located in an area with several other hotels nearby, but we believe that what we have to offer is a better solution for travelers than what they can find elsewhere. We listen to people's frustrations and provide a better answer.

If guests need a hotel van to take them to the airport 24 hours a day, 7 days a week, we offer that service. Everything is based on meeting the customer's needs better than anyone else—not just because we are competitive but because we strive to be sensitive to God's love for the people who come to our door.

3. We help foster a strong sense of community

When the Jesuits and other missionaries came to America, they were ambassadors of mission entrepreneurialism. We don't usually think of them as MBEs, but we know that their missions were faith-based businesses. Those missions became the hub of the local economy in addition to the place where people came with the sick and dying. The missions built a strong sense of community all week long. They didn't shut down after the Sunday message. The mission was always open. We aim to do the same with our hotel-church.

4. We create systems designed for success

One of the reasons that some faith-based businesses fail is the leader's lack of commitment to the systems that make a business successful. A pastor or Christian leader sometimes has developed habits of spiritual spontaneity that are much like the typical entrepreneur, always wanting to do something bigger and better. Some of that energy is good. However, he can still leave room for innovation if he hires managers and runs the business by systematic practices that are always careful- ly followed. At a hotel, for example, guests expect certain housekeeping practices to occur in a timely manner every day. They want the service to be not only excellent but predictable.

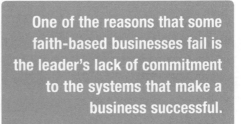

One of the reasons that some faith-based businesses fail is the leader's lack of commitment to the systems that make a business successful.

One of the advantages of following systems is that some days the business seems to run itself. You can enjoy the adventure instead of struggling with the breakdowns, detail by detail. You also provide a feeling of peace and order for your staff and customers alike when they know that certain procedures will be followed. You want them to feel good when they walk away.

5. We hire and train only committed people

It takes commitment to run a successful business venture. Sometimes your commitment pays off, sometimes it needs to go the extra mile. One morning shortly after we had bought our hotel I was working at the hotel's front desk and a man called to ask for towels. I couldn't find any! Any linen supply I saw was stained and torn as we had inherited it from the previous owner. The new supply we had ordered hadn't come in yet. I scrambled around and finally found some hand towels and took them to his room. It was all I could think of to do.

"These aren't towels, you idiot!" he said. He had come soaking wet from the shower and was dripping wet. But there were no clean towels anywhere in our hotel! That was a learning opportunity for me, both to have committed people on board and also to have committed systems in place.

When we inherited our hotel we were short on both. We didn't terminate the former staff, as a few were good workers and we wanted to change things slowly. Over time we hired our own team who we trained in our own systems; systems based on commitment and excellence.

When we set out on this mission, we didn't begin by establishing a lot of job descriptions either. We began with a dream that we could make a difference in people's lives. We created an environment of inspiration that became contagious. If you asked many of the church and staff members how they feel about this work, they would tell you this is one of the best experiences of their lives. We are on a wild ride with lots of challenges and many times we fall short, but we can't think of anything else we would rather do.

On Sunday mornings Rita and I stand before our congregation together to bring them greetings. New people see a husband and wife team who not only love one another but love those whom God brings to us at our "mission station." Those who labor with us see that we are consistent in our commitment to our marriage as well as our work.

Because we believe in the Bible and use it to govern our lives and our business, we can operate according to worthwhile standards and full integrity. We have built a sense of relationship with one another that is different from the isolation experienced by many people today. Although not everyone who comes here is willing to be accountable to our standards or submit to our oversight, we believe in functioning as a family. Those who are ordained to be with us embrace that.

I love people and I love this church and business. It is fun to be here. Every week brings something I never knew was going to happen. Every weekend is different. I hate to be away from this place because it is such a great adventure.

Although I would love to tell you that everyone who works here is like Jeff, whom you met earlier, the truth of the matter is that like any place, there are those who have not caught the dream. For them it is a job, but for the rest of us, we believe in servanthood. We work as hard as we can because the rewards are great. We have rolled up our sleeves and gone to work and lives have been changed as a result.

6. We rely on faith

One of the women in the ladies' ministry, Helen, is now in her eighties. She doesn't sit around wondering if there is anything left to do at her age. She is an intercessor—not only for the church but also for the hotel staff and the guests who come through our doors each year. Each week Helen and other ladies lovingly handwrite personal greetings inside the covers of paperback NIV Bibles. Then they place them in the hotel rooms for our guests to read and take away with them. They have faith that some of those people will find a new life because the ladies took the time to pray and write those words.

In the early days of the hotel, small victories sustained our faith. We would purposely look for anything that would give us a sense of gratitude to God for allowing us to work in this place. We might fall into bed exhausted at night, but each morning we awoke with a sense of excitement that some new miracle would occur before the day was out. Gradually we developed greater endurance to face the inevitable setbacks and adversity. We learned how to encourage one another in the Lord.

In order to operate a faith-based business, you need a lot of faith! Even if you see obstacles ahead, you have to believe that you can overcome them. Maybe others have failed, but you are convinced you are not like them. You're an incurable optimist. No matter how bad it gets, you believe a solution is right around the corner. You refuse to accept impossibilities. You follow the sense of direction from your inner spirit. The Bible says, "Therefore encourage one another and build each other up, just as in fact you are doing."[2]

7. We aim to consistently operate on Christ-like principles

A century ago a Congregational minister named Charles Sheldon wrote a book that became one of the best-selling novels of all time, *In His Steps*. It was the fictional account of a pastor named Henry Maxwell in a town called Raymond. This pastor was confronted by his own lack of concern for those in need when a homeless man came to his church, collapsed and died. He challenged himself and members of his congregation to live their everyday lives according to the question, "What would Jesus do?"

The real-life Sheldon not only wrote about compassion; he also lived it. He grew up in the Dakota Territory among Native Americans and had a love for people of all races and classes, especially those whose lives were shattered by prejudice. He did everything he could to meet the needs of others. His motivation was not just kindness. He was a man who prayed and read the Bible daily and was driven by the force of God in his life.

When Sheldon started his first pastorate in Waterbury, Connecticut, he began a career of faith-based businesses when he planted a vegetable garden on church land and sold the produce. In 1889, he became the founding pastor of Central Congregational Church in Topeka, Kansas, where he would spend the rest of his life. The Topeka church began in a small room over a butcher's shop where he preached a bold message about a Christ who loves all people. Meanwhile, unemployment was escalating. He found that churches in the area were unsympathetic, blaming the unemployed for laziness. Deciding to launch his personal undercover investigation, Sheldon disguised himself as a worker in old clothes. He went looking for work but could find none. He saw firsthand that it was not the fault of the unemployed.

Sheldon lived among people from different races and social groups in Topeka. As a result, he was the first White person to say openly that the poverty of the poor and especially Blacks, was not incompetence but oppression. He also boldly spoke out against the Ku Klux Klan.

When he opened social services for the local population and started a kindergarten, other churches became involved. Crime fell. Alcoholism decreased. The youth loved coming to his church and many dedicated their lives to becoming missionaries.

YOUR CONSUMING FOCUS

What Sheldon did is what we want to accomplish in our church. We would hope it is also what you want to accomplish in your mission. We want to train and release ordinary people who have been with Jesus to influence and transform their communities through business, government, education, media and the arts. We want to become the undisputed leader in the development and implementation of a servant entrepreneurial model within the hospitality industry for the local, national and global Church. We hope to plant hundreds of churches through a multiplication process and be a church that never closes its doors. We want to undertake the ministry of Christ's compassion and care through involvement in social issues and intentional outreach to the surrounding community.

We are the Church.

We are not people who go to church on Sunday and live another life on Monday morning. There is no distinction between church and hotel and what we do in our everyday lives. We are open 24/7. We never close. We are here to meet the needs of others by love. And that really is the driving focus of our mission: love.

On the night before Jesus was crucified, His final instructions to His followers were about love. He said, "Love one another and then others will know that you follow Me."[3] That simple command transcended anything that other world leaders have said or say today. Jesus told His followers to change the world by love. Not military conquest or political intrigue, but love. His words were understated, yet powerful. He didn't say to restrict our love only to other Christians or people who look and act like us. He said to love everybody—especially those who are different—and if we did, their lives would be changed forever.

How about you? Are you changing your community by love? In any significant endeavor that God calls you to launch, your love for the people around you will be tested. There will be times when you want to quit and you are not sure you can take another step. But it can be done. I encourage you to immerse yourself in the realities of your dream.

SUMMARY

+ What is it like trying to run a business on faith-based terms? Becoming an MBE means you and your team will be called upon to respond to a variety of situations with Christ-like grace.

+ Think of today's Christ-centered MBE ventures as modern mission outposts, places that help, encourage, refresh and train people to lead new lives.

+ Seven commitments will allow you to succeed at both your mission and your business:

1. Respect your paying guests.
2. Have a unique product and offer consistent outstanding customer service.
3. Help foster a strong sense of community.
4. Hire and train only committed people.
5. Create systems designed for success.
6. Rely on faith.
7. Aim to consistently operate on Christ-like principles.

CHAPTER SEVEN

HANG ON TO YOUR PARTNERS

A middle-aged mother and father were at home one evening when they received a telephone call from their recently married daughter. The father picked up the receiver. For some time all he heard were tears, anger and frustration. It was his daughter on the line. The newlyweds had their first big fight.

After about half an hour of active listening, the father rejoined the mother on the couch.

"Well, what happened?" asked the mother.

"She said she wanted to come home," the father replied.

"What did you tell her?"

"I told her she *was* home."[1]

When a blacksmith forges a piece of metal, he heats it in the fire until it is no longer hard. Then he can hammer it into shape. Because of the fire, the metal is less likely to fracture when he pounds it again and again. In the same way, those who set out to accomplish a great mission must forge strong relationships with the people God brings into their lives, just as a blacksmith forges metal. That means you have to be willing to be changed by other people every day.

Working through tears, anger and frustration—either literally or metaphorically—is part of any healthy and strong partnership. Building strong relationships of trust in family, church and business is critical to any endeavor of life, but especially when you are trying to advance the Kingdom as an MBE. Ministry and business can be tough teachers. If you want to be a successful MBE you need to adopt the maxim that "quitting isn't an option" when it comes to two key relationships: your marriage and your business partners. Differing opinions will always exist, but you'll need those key relationships to take you through the tough times when your dream seems to have turned dark and you can't find a way out.

> If you want to be a successful MBE you need to adopt the maxim that "quitting isn't an option" when it comes to two key relationships: your marriage and your business partners.

In this chapter, we'll show you some valuable tools for learning to get along with your strongest allies while pursuing your dream. Building strong relationships of trust in family, church and business is critical to any endeavor of life, but especially when you are trying to advance your mission. Ministry and business can be tough teachers. If you aspire to be an MBE, look around and thank God for the people He has placed in your life and forge a strong family unity.

THE KEY PARTNERSHIP: YOUR MARRIAGE

Though MBE's are typically very driven individuals, it will take a family to realize your vision. In our push to create a church-hotel venture, my wife Rita has always stood by me. She has been a great source of strength and healing in my life. After working all day, most people would give up and leave the dishes in the sink. She doesn't do that. She will work to the point of total exhaustion. Some women won't push on into the night the way she does. Many nights she would work setting up new guest rooms, planting flowers and pressure washing the outside of the walkways of the hotel until very late into the night. Then she would drive home and take care of household chores such as laundry before falling into bed at 3 am. God knew what we would have to go through to accomplish His purposes and He knew that if it all depended on Eric and his dreams it would never happen.

With any God-sized dream you always have challenges and doubts. Sometimes you question if the dream came from God in the first place. You are in the middle of a disaster and the dream is caving in around you. When you are $1.5 million short of funds for necessary renovations and $600 thousand short on operational income, as we were, it is easy to despair. In hard times like that it would be tempting to throw in the towel and call it quits, but I learned early on in my marriage that quitting isn't an option when times get hard. What I know now in hindsight is that God was preparing us all along for a greater calling. The hard times early on in our marriage were part of the blacksmith process. God was solidifying our marriage into the strongest entity possible.

It didn't seem that way at the time though. When I married Rita, I know now that I did not have a clue about what marriage was all about. We were married on June 15, 1986 and by that September we were at seminary. By November I thought I had made a big mistake. I don't remember what the argument in November was all about and neither does my wife, but whatever it was it had escalated beyond reason. Everything seemed monumental when we were just starting out. We had little furniture and even less money. We lived in a small one-bedroom apartment in student housing with brown shag carpet and orange furniture. The walls were so thin that when I brushed my teeth I could carry on a conversation through the medicine cabinet with the guy next door.

Since I was in school to earn a master's degree in divinity to become a pastor, I knew that it said in the Bible, "Don't let the sun go down on your anger,"[2] but we didn't follow that. When we had an argument we stayed mad and didn't speak for days. I could never figure out how to say, "I'm sorry." When you are young twenty-somethings, everything can feel overwhelming. After five months, I felt as if I had lost my freedom. I couldn't go out with the guys the way I used to or do the things I did in college. You see, I was still in a cycle where life was all about me and what I wanted. Some people in life never lose this edge. I decided that my only option was divorce.

I made an appointment to talk to Dwight Nelson, senior pastor of the seminary church. He had a large whiteboard on his wall. When I told him that I had made a mistake and wanted a divorce, he started laughing out loud. To me it was the end of world, but he said basically, "Get a grip, Eric." Then, on the whiteboard he wrote one verse from the Bible, "Husbands, love your wives, just as Christ loved the Church and gave Himself up for her."[3] He said, "When Jesus gave His life for you and me, we didn't deserve what He gave us. He was the ultimate servant. He was willing to die." Then he shocked me. He said, "Eric, when you are the husband, you need to be the strong one who takes the first step toward forgiveness and says 'I'm sorry.' You have to become like Christ. It's no longer about you. It's about her. Marriage is designed to kill you. You have to die."

I looked at him in total disbelief and burst out, "But that isn't fair!"

He said, "You're right. Marriage isn't fair. It's designed to forge a man of character. After you said 'I do' you died. Your life is no longer about your rights and what you want. It has to be about her needs now. Get used to it. Anything that lasts cannot be built upon your own selfish desires. Be grateful that God isn't fair. If He was, we would all be lost. Jesus took your place. His strength of character as a man allowed Him to empty Himself for you. He made Himself of no reputation.[4] You have to do that for Rita. That is the secret to opening her heart. You are there to serve her and be her support. It won't always be fair, but she will open up to you like a flower and you will see her woman's heart turn toward you. You need to go back and get some flowers and say you're sorry."

As I walked out of his office on that cold winter morning, I sensed I had just learned something that would change my life. My situation with Rita had not changed, but my thinking had. Something inside me had been altered and I felt as though I had just been given the greatest gift a man could ever receive. Wisdom. Only one question now remained. Would it really work? I quickly made my way to the store and bought her some flowers and a teddy bear holding a handkerchief with the words "I'm sorry" on it and a tear falling down his face. I put it on the dresser with the flowers before Rita got home.

When she came in the door, I was working at my computer. She didn't say anything to me because we were still not talking. The apartment was so tiny that I could hear her go into the bedroom and then I heard her start to cry. I went in and said, "I'm sorry," and she said, "I am, too." That was the best advice I ever got. We're still married 23 years later.

That was an important principle of forging family unity, whether in my home, my extended family or my other relationships. I had to be willing to ask forgiveness first. Life isn't about me. This is a hard lesson for people to learn and the more I'm around others the more I realize how few have learned this lesson. It isn't something you learn with your head. It has to be something you feel in your heart. Relationships will wound you, but as Benjamin Franklin said, "The things which hurt, instruct."[5] You can do better next time. You won't always get it right, but you can always keep trying because that is what makes you strong. You don't have to fix everything. You can even forget wrongs if you ask for forgiveness and move on.

These days when Rita and I have one of our "discussions" and I say things I wish I hadn't said and she says things she shouldn't have said, we don't hold on to it because we learned that doesn't work. Most of the time we just forget it and move on. We have learned to give one another the gift of grace, as Jesus did for us.

THE VITAL LINK IN YOUR MISSION

Whenever people come together, inevitably you will have tension. In marriage, ministry, business, getting an education or whatever dream you go after, there will be times when you just don't see eye to eye. People who leave relationships because they can't stand the heat lose the benefit of the fires that make you strong. When you follow the pattern of God's grace and grant people space when they offend you, you can build the kind of relationships that everyone needs to grow. You learn to love and forgive them and look for the best in one another.

The Bible says that love "keeps no records of wrongs."[6] In other words, love doesn't keep an injury scorecard. If you keep track of offenses against you, your relationships won't work. If you get mad every time you're not thanked or recognized, you will never feel fulfilled. Unless you want God keeping a scorecard on you, give others some grace.

If she said something awful, she probably didn't mean it that way. If he hurt your feelings, it's okay. We must have honesty and transparency with each other and we won't always say things perfectly and we need to give others the same kind of honor that we would like to receive. Scott Peck, M.D. wrote, "It is in this whole process of meeting and solving problems that life has meaning. Problems are the cutting edge that distinguishes between success and failure. Problems call forth our courage and our wisdom; indeed, they create our courage and our wisdom. It is only because of problems that we grow mentally and spiritually. . . . It is through the pain of confronting and resolving problems that we learn."[7]

Forgiveness is key in this process. In his book, *Lee: The Last Years,* author Charles Bracelen Flood reports that after the Civil War, Robert E. Lee visited a Kentucky lady who took him to the remains of a grand old tree in front of her house. There she bitterly cried that much of its limbs and trunk had been destroyed by Federal artillery fire. She looked to Lee for a word condemning the North or at least sympathizing with her loss. After a brief silence, Lee said, "Cut it down, my dear Madam and forget it." His point was that it's better to forgive the injustices of the past than to allow them to remain and let bitterness take root and poison the rest of our lives.[8]

I encourage you to thank God for and honor the people He has placed in your life. He knew you would need them to help you be the leader you are today. Together you are much stronger than you ever would have been apart. If you can't do what is necessary to forge family unity, first and business unity second, you might as well close this book. Your dreams will be dashed and your fortitude will fracture. When the going gets tough, you'll want to quit. However, if you will forge family unity by staying in the fire, you will be able to survive the incredibly difficult moments of sheer terror that lie ahead and gain a deeper love for the people God has placed in your life.

SERVANT POWER

The same skills you need to sharpen to serve your spouse are what God employs to serve your customers and those who need a Savior. Do you have limits on what you will do for others? How far will you go to show someone Jesus through your life? Acts of service are not performed in the vacuum of a life that has not been forged in the furnace of affliction. If life is all about you, it will be difficult for you to really love.

For instance, in the early days of the hotel, a man went on an all-night drinking binge in one of our rooms. The housekeepers saw an example of a servant leader in my wife when she helped the house-keepers clean up the bathroom where he threw up. We didn't believe in making someone else do what we were unwilling to do ourselves. We were not divided by race or social standing. We did the tough jobs together. Those experiences forged unity and developed our love for one another.

Shortly after this incident, an older couple came and stayed with us for several months. The wife was handicapped and used a wheel-chair. She couldn't get out of bed by herself. They paid for their room, so that was not a problem, but it was the extra care that our hotel staff gave that was extraordinary. The lady couldn't get up when her husband was gone so sometimes she would mess the bed. Not one housekeeper said, "Handicapped people are not my job. I'm not a nursing home attendant, you know. I'm a housekeeper. You don't pay me to help a woman get into her wheelchair and clean her up when she messes her bed sheets." They never said that. They served the public, they served us and ultimately they served God.

When Jesus left behind a small group of followers and said, "Go and make disciples," they obeyed Him by taking care of one another and reaching out to others. They made disciples by becoming an example of Jesus Himself. That is what we have to do here. We have to be willing to serve. It's not about us. It's about others. We are all God's children. Unless you have a servant's mentality, it will be almost impossible to make a mission-based enterprise work, especially in the hospitality business. If you focus on what's fair to you or how you can get rich and famous, this is not for you. First you must have a servant's heart. You can't look down on people as if they are less than you. That is how you forge family unity.

> **Unless you have a servant's mentality, it will be almost impossible to make a mission-based enterprise work, especially in the hospitality business.**

One boundary we needed to cross was our relationship with homeless people. When we had remodeled the hotel enough to move in new furniture, we hired some help from Labor Ready, a temporary labor pool. That was how we met Dusty, a giving man in his fifties who happened to be homeless.

Dusty was a heavy smoker and he couldn't seem to stop coughing. He asked lots of questions about the church. He didn't come from the same background as we did and his appearance was much like many of the guys you would find on the corner of a busy intersection holding a sign and asking for money or trying to warm himself on the streets of an inner city. The only difference is that Dusty wanted to try and earn his money.

Someone invited Dusty to church. At the close of the service, I asked if anyone would like to start a new relationship with Christ and Dusty raised his hand. That day we were holding our first baptism in the hotel's outdoor swimming pool and Dusty decided to be baptized. He walked up the outdoor steps to the pool, carefully took off his shirt and shoes, then walked right in with his clothes on. In some circles that would have been an awkward moment, but you could see that Dusty knew in his heart that he wanted to change his life. Nothing was going to get in the way, including church tradition. It is easy to misjudge the Dustys of the world if you don't see the person behind the exterior and just think of them as homeless bums who don't want to work. A family is made up of "all kinds of people" from all different walks of life. Today, Dusty is no longer homeless and both he and his mother attend our church together.

Another barrier can come from interactions with people from different cultures. In the hospitality industry, some people look down on immigrant workers because they usually hold the jobs that no one else wants, such as housekeeping. Even in the church, people can look down on other race and judge people by the color of their skin, their educational level or their socio-economic status, even if they won't admit it. That is not the way a real family functions. When the church and the business are operated like a family, you never look down on people.

When the hotel started, I saw the potential of a relationship gap between the Hispanic housekeepers and the rest of the staff if something didn't happen to change people's attitudes. Not long after we took over the hotel, we encountered a situation in one of the hotel rooms that was beyond any vandalism I could have imagined. Some guests had smeared fecal matter everywhere. The filth was caked all over the walls, ground into the carpet and smeared over the sheets. It was disgusting.

Rita was the head housekeeper at the time. She was management, so to speak. She wasn't responsible for cleaning rooms, so that mess was not her job. One of the housekeepers had that assignment, but since Rita doesn't believe that she is better than anyone else, regardless of their nationality or skin color, she rolled up her sleeves and she the other housekeeper covered their faces and went to work.

They threw away the sheets and scrubbed the carpets and walls. When they had finished, you couldn't tell that room from any other. It was spotless.

My wife changed the way people in our ministry and staff looked at those of another culture. She loved them and supported them as family. She praised them for the way they were willing to go into the worst environments and do their jobs. By her example, she helped set the standard of humility for the others. She showed that none of us is too good to serve—especially when someone messes up your house.

ROOTS OF DESTINY

Whatever the situation is with your family of origin, I believe that God strategically placed you in that family for a reason. I know in my own life the ability that my wife and I have for treating people like family whenever they show up at the door is partly the result of our family backgrounds. We didn't begin our lives together when Eastside Foursquare Church bought the hotel. We brought with us experiences from the past that had already shaped our lives. We approached this opportunity from the perspective of a family that was making the hotel an extension of our home and our church. Those hotel guests would be our guests.

Rita is a hard worker in part because of her German parents. I am familiar with people who have never attended church because of my dad and mom, Billy and Vicky Bahme, who are a product of the sixties' culture. God uses the environment where we grew up, no matter how difficult things seemed to be at the time, to prepare us for our future. What I received from my parents' DNA is helping me reach out to people in need. Mom and Dad didn't attend church when I was growing up. In fact, when I was born she and my father had just gotten married. Their generation believed in free love. They got married and raised me in an environment of drinking and drugs, but somehow known only to God I found Jesus and they did, too.

Two years ago, I baptized my mother in the swimming pool at the hotel. She looked around at the beautiful campus restoration and the kind of needy people we were reaching and she told me, "Everything you have done here, you were destined to do. I can see it. You had no choice." In some ways my upbringing in the post-sixties environment actually gave me more sensitivity to people with substance abuse problems. It helped prepare me to work with the people I meet in this inner-city neighborhood every day. My mom told me, "If you hadn't been raised in that type of home environment, you probably couldn't do this." She was right. My parents' lifestyle helped create in me a sense of compassion and a lack of judgment toward all kinds of people. God has built a Church that is different from anything that my wife and I had ever been a part of before in mainstream religion. It's as big as God's love and I believe it most clearly reflects the model of the early Church.

Paul said in 1 Corinthians 13 that the greatest gift is love. You reach people first by love, not rules. The standards come later, but first they have to know that you care about them. When Christians lay aside our differences and work together to fulfill the Gospel commission by loving people as family, that is when we will be able to change the world.

WHEN SACRIFICES BECOME JOYS

In building your MBE venture, your family may need to sacrifice certain things that other families often take for granted. But those very same things you sacrifice may turn out to be opportunities for some of your greatest joys.

For us, we needed to sacrifice a single-family house. To explain, my immediate family consists of my wife and our daughter Alyssa. We live with our extended family. Together we share a home and support a common vision for Eastside —two families living peaceably together. My wife and I and our daughter live in the same house with my wife's sister Judy Grambow, who manages the coffee shop called

Sacred Grounds Espresso at Eastside, her husband, Jeff, and their two sons, Brian and Kristofer.

Our two families are committed to this dream, but we knew there would be a significant price to pay. Anytime you embark on a great dream, often the family pays the greatest price. In a new business or a start-up church, if the family doesn't buy into the vision and isn't a part of the work, it can destroy them. You can't focus on gaining the world so much that you lose your own soul—and your family.

We decided to forge this partnership because we wanted to be sure that someone would always be there when the kids got home from school. We wanted to have dinner together every night, even if we were working crazy hours and not everyone could make it on time. We knew it would take four adults to create a stable home environment because of all the demands this ministry would require.

No business or ministry is so important that it is worth destroying your family. God created families. The family is also the basic foundation for both church and business. I have seen families torn apart too many times. It doesn't have to end that way. You can forge family unity in the midst of building a business or church by making sure there is lots of love to go around and your spouse and children are involved in the new endeavor.

> You can't focus on gaining the world so much that you lose your own soul—and your family.

My brother-in-law, Jeff, travels with his job outside the ministry, but whenever he's in town you can count on him to work at the hotel or take care of projects at home. My nephew, Brian, started volunteering at the hotel when he was 15, tearing out old rooms, cleaning up old hypodermic needles on campus, doing odd jobs and working at the front desk. He worked his way up to become assistant manager for a summer. Today he is a student at the Cornell University School of Hotel Management in Ithaca, New York and is preparing for a future in the ministry.

One night when Brian and I were working at the front desk, a guest called to complain about how the beds had been made. We went to the room and the people were very gracious. They saw two guys who looked as if they didn't know which way to turn the sheets and they gave us more credit than we deserved. I'm not sure if the beds looked much better after we got through with them but we tried and we had a good time doing it together as a family.

My nephew, Kristofer, also helped rebuild the facility and is one of our paid baristas in the coffee shop, Sacred Grounds Espresso, where 42,000 customers passed through last year. Even my daughter, Alyssa, has helped either with dishes in the coffee shop or working with her mom in projects around the hotel.

As a family we have experienced the good times and the bad in this project. We have been a part of seeing God do something that is truly a miracle and we have left a legacy for our children to see how God moves. Our children have not just heard about God's provision. They have experienced it.

We are amazed today to see how big this has become! With each passing day it gets even larger, but we will never forget how it all began. You can never teach lessons like these to your children without experiencing them together, working side by side. Living, laughing, crying and moving through the process of a dream being fulfilled. Our children understand that with God you can dream, with God you can see things come about. They also know that it takes hard work. Life isn't easy, even if the call is from God, but when you keep it real your marriage stays strong and hearts are knitted together. I'm glad our children have learned that life isn't fair because it has taught them how to fight for what they believe in.

Our extended family couldn't be more committed to giving themselves to this dream. These experiences embed themselves into the lives of your children, your church and your community. Working together in good times and bad builds character and shapes an emerging generation for their own destiny.

Part of the joy comes from the ability to laugh together. One day, in preparation for some great church volunteers who would come to move in new furniture, we needed to dispose of the old, stained stuff that we had inherited when we bought the hotel. We didn't want to spend a lot of money at the dump, so I came up with the idea of asking Brian and Kristofer to stand on the corner of our property with signs saying "Free Furniture!"

Within minutes, the hotel parking lot was packed with cars! It was a stampede. Like a plague of locusts, the neighborhood descended upon the place. Hundreds of people were rushing up and down the outdoor stairways, bumping into one another, getting into fights, going in and out of rooms, carrying out everything in sight. It didn't matter how bad the stuff looked. They would pile it on top of their cars or cram in into their open trunks and drive away. One guy left carrying a nightstand on a bike. They emptied more than 40 rooms of furniture in what seemed like minutes. We laugh about those stories when our family sits around the dinner table.

One night Rita and Judy were working late to clean up the day's construction mess by pressure-washing the second-story walkways. Suddenly they saw a man below walking along as though he owned the place. He was looking into the windows of several units that were vacant at the time because they were being renovated. He had a metal briefcase in his hand. He didn't pay much attention to them, probably because he didn't know who they were. Rita and Judy grew up in a family of hard-working German immigrants who would tackle anything. When they saw the strange man below, they didn't panic. They decided that Judy would go and find Dave, our children's pastor who was also the front office manager for the hotel, while Rita kept an eye on the stranger. After all, she still held the pressure washer in her hand.

Dave came right out. He walked over to the man and said firmly, "I'm sorry, but you will have to leave." The man took his time moving on and then stopped right around the corner. He seemed to have no sense that he was about to be apprehended. Dave called the police. When they arrived, the man was still hanging around, so they arrested him. We had heard about a string of car thefts at nearby hotels that the police had been unable to solve. They never told us what was in that metal briefcase, but from that day on there were no more car thefts. Not all crime-solvers are men. Some are strong sisters.

THE NECESSITY OF UNITY

Sometimes families are blood relatives but at other times a family is a group of people with similar beliefs and convictions, like a church family. At Eastside Foursquare Church, we have many wonderful servants with the grace of God on their lives. We consider ourselves "family." We have been through some significant moments together. Just like any family, we go through good times and bad but we don't give up on one another.

Divorce is not an option in marriage and neither is "divorcing" the people whom God gives you in other important relationships. People will say and do things they don't mean or that you misinterpret. People will rub you the wrong way and you will rub them the wrong way, but you need those relationships to take you through the tough times when your dream seems to have turned dark and you can't find a way out.

Because of the type of church that we have created, people come and go. We are all about touching lives and thousands pass through our doors every year. Some people who come to a church service may be traveling through. Others may come from the neighborhood with a substance abuse problem, but for various reasons not everyone can be a permanent member. However, we always have a core of committed people to carry on the ministry and provide a stable church family that is not going anywhere.

Before we bought the hotel, David Walmer and his wife, Arly, joined us in this dream. Since then, David has done many jobs at Eastside from executive pastor to general manager of the hotel. He has been stretched and challenged in new ways. He is not only a close friend but also a faithful person who has demonstrated loyalty and perseverance. David doesn't quit when the going gets tough. Over the years we have had some disagreements on how things should be done, but we have never given up on our relationship. Many times he has convinced me that I was going in the wrong direction and saved me from making a big mistake because I humbled myself and took his advice.

So many people have faithfully served here at Eastside that it would be impossible to name them all or to even begin to do justice in recognition of their service—folding laundry, cleaning rooms, planting flowers, driving the shuttle, working the front desk—the list is endless.

Like a marriage, church departments sometimes fight one another over small things that aren't even important. People can get their feelings hurt so easily when they don't see the big picture. Maybe they both need the church van on the same day and only one gets to use it so the other one goes to find a new church. Or someone will say, "This church is just using me. They are always taking advantage of me." Then they go find another pastor.

Some people feel that they aren't being used at all and can't understand why someone else is chosen and they are not. Others get wounded because they aren't paid for their work. Years later, after they have left the church and ruined relationships with people they once cared about, the incident may seem petty, like my first big argument with my wife. They can't even remember what it was about. How much better it would be to stay together and forgive.

It took a family to build this place—not only my wife and in-laws but also the Eastside Church family and other churches. People came from all over to help us tear out old carpets, strip walls and pull out old toilets and sinks and throw them away. Senior pastors left their churches to work on the construction to make a dream come alive.

Eventually, we had to replace almost everything in the hotel down to the studs. Like the new lives God was creating in us, everything became brand new. Finally, after we rebuilt the plumbing and the electrical wiring and the neighbors had trucked away the old furniture, it was time to move in the new furniture. Twenty or thirty people volunteered to steam drapes, make beds, hang pictures and headboards and move in the coffee pots. When we didn't have money to hire enough housekeepers, we cleaned some of the rooms ourselves. We drove the van for the airport shuttle. Everyone on staff had to pitch in at one time or another. We were poor but we were a family working together to fulfill a dream.

Every guest whose life we now touch—whether by personal contact with hotel staff, reading one of our Bibles, attending a church service or being served in the coffee shop—would never have been reached without the commitment of this family. I passionately love these people. When I see them, I see sacrifice.

I am committed to my family—my wife, daughter, in-laws and the whole Eastside Foursquare Church family—regardless of where they are in the development process. We live together, we minister together and we work in a business together. All of us are willing to serve one another. It's not all about us. It's all about God and the people He wants us to reach. In the world there are racial and economic chasms, but the Church should be a family. Some of the people who come through our doors may not smell so good. They may not act "normal" or they may not say things the right way, but we still welcome them into the family.

As hard as this hotel project has been for us, there is something about building the mission together that forges unity. We are deeply ingrained as a family because we have worked side by side. We have emerged from the flames stronger—not only for ourselves but also for people in crisis who arrive at our door. Without those experiences, we would not have the courage to be Christians who offer pastoral ministry to hotel guests accustomed to living in a secular society.

SUMMARY

✚ When you set out to build an MBE enterprise, you must forge strong relationships with the people God brings into your life.

✚ Building strong relationships of trust in family, church and business is critical to any endeavor of life, but especially as an MBE. If you want to be a successful MBE you need to adopt the maxim that "quitting isn't an option" when it comes to your marriage and your business partners. Differing opinions will always exist, but you'll need those key relationships to take you through the tough times when your dream seems to have turned dark and you can't find a way out.

✚ When you and your spouse disagree, be the first to ask forgiveness. After an argument or misunderstanding, keep no record of wrongs.

✚ Adopt the attitude of servant leadership with employees and partners.

✚ No business or ministry is so important that it is worth destroying your family. God created families. The family is also the basic foundation for both church and business. Forge family unity in the midst of building a business or mission by making sure there is lots of love to go around and that your spouse and children are involved in your new endeavor.

✚ Some of the greatest challenges in your MBE venture will turn out to be the greatest joys.

CHAPTER EIGHT

THE VITAL CONSTANT

There's one vital component behind all successful MBE ventures that I want to emphasize as you develop your dream. It's excellence. Excellence leads to influence—and that's the real business we're in—influencing people's lives for good.

Sometimes as leaders of non-profits and churches, we have in mind that because we're not in the business of making money, then whatever is second best will do. Organizations sometimes adopt a folksy mentality where the leaders expect the patrons to acquiesce to sub-standard programs, buildings, staffing and services. This should not be.

Whatever your dream is, you must adopt the attitude of excellence in all you do. Your mission is to help people better their lives and when your mission involves something as important as that, excellence is the only operating paradigm that will work.

THE ROOTS OF EXCELLENCE

As I was developing my dream, I discovered this deeper model for reaching people through excellent acts of hospitable service. It happened when I met the man behind the success of the Ritz-Carlton, which for years was the number one luxury hotel brand in the world.

Many people do not realize that Horst Schulze, considered the leading hotelier worldwide, is a dedicated Christian. He served 14 years as the Ritz-Carlton's president, COO and vice chairman. Then in 2002, he left to become president and chief executive officer of the

West Paces Hotel Group, which includes Capella Hotels, the world's first six-star hotel brand and Solís, a luxury chain competing with Four Seasons and the Ritz-Carlton.

When Schulze was approached to lead the company by the owners of the Ritz-Carlton in the early 1980s, he turned them down many times. Eventually in 1983 he said he would come on board only if they gave him complete liberty to do whatever he wanted. He built the brand on biblical principles of serving people and treating them well. His customer service motto became "Ladies and gentlemen serving ladies and gentlemen," the idea that respect and service would originate with staff and extend to all customers.

Schulze developed a variety of systems, most still in place, that help employees do their jobs well and provide a consistent experience of excellence for hotel guests. When something went wrong during the course of business, he did not fault the employee. He fixed the system.

From the first time I met Schulze a few years ago, he has graciously been another mentor to me. He is a biblical entrepreneur like Joseph in the Bible and exemplifies the eight qualities of an MBE that you read about earlier in this book. One afternoon after a speaking engagement in Atlanta that he had graciously invited me to attend, we were roaring down the Atlanta freeway in his Mercedes as if we were on the Autobahn. He handed me a folded, laminated card that described the mission of his organization. He and his employees always carry it with them. He said to me passionately in his German accent, "I want everyone to know what our mission is at all times. We are all about excellence! Your job as a leader, Eric, is also to let people know why you're in business and what is required. You must be clear."

Schulze let me keep his card. I not only read his credo, mission statement, code of conduct and principles of service; I also decided to carry it with me every day. It reminds me to strive for excellence in my own life and it challenges me to be a better pastor, leader and businessman.

Most people would say that the Ritz-Carlton is a world away from the Church's reality—a difference of night and day—but I believe if the church can raise its standards and get rid of its poverty thinking, we can experience new levels of success. We can get a vision for true prosperity that covers every area and then implement that vision in daily life as we seek to help people live better lives, spiritually, physically, mentally and emotionally.

I can't help but wonder what a man like Schulze could do around the board table in the church. He knows how to build and operate hotels with a level of excellence that is world class. He has raised billions of dollars to make his vision of the world's premier hotel chain come true. He has a passion to serve others better than anyone else. He knows how to transform a community and carries the living, loving Jesus inside of him. He

> Most people would say that the Ritz-Carlton is a world away from the Church's reality—a difference of night and day—but I believe if the church can raise its standards and get rid of its poverty thinking, we can experience new levels of success.

has blessed my life with great wisdom and has been available to me whenever I have had questions. That day in his car he told me that he would build the number one hotel chain in the world and I believe he will.

The vital constant with Schulze is excellence. Excellence leads to influence. That is our vital constant at Eastside and I hope it is yours as well. Let's take a look at some of the practical ways that this formula plays out in daily life.

THE REASONS FOR EXCELLENCE

At the Portland Airport Quality Inn and Suites and Rodeway Inn in Portland Oregon, we consistently meet and often exceed the standards of the hospitality chain with which we are affiliated. People love to stay in our hotels and they even take the time to record their approval ratings on the Internet for everyone else to see. They tell their friends about us. As of this writing, our Quality Inn and Suites is ranked number 30 out of 810 Quality Inn and Suites internationally and our Rodeway is 15 out of 270. Both properties are Gold Award properties, meaning they fall into the top 10 percent of the brand. When we purchased our properties they were near the bottom of the list, so the point is that we've rapidly moved up. I'm happy with our rankings, but I'm not completely satisfied. These are God's hotels. They both need to be number 1. That's the mentality we need to have as Christians.

Some people—even Christians—are afraid that a business guided by faith will drive people away, but it actually drives traffic to us because we are so committed to customer service. We run our business in such a way that our customers see us as an example of Christ-likeness whether we mention His name or not. We treat everyone who comes through the door as if they were Jesus and we were meeting Jesus' needs. That's a level of service people remember!

> Some people—even Christians—are afraid that a business guided by faith will drive people away, but it actually drives traffic to us because we are so committed to customer service.

Why do we consistently strive for excellence? James pointed out in the Bible that "faith without works is dead."[1] We can use our good works to reach people by using actions that speak louder than words. Of course, we also make sure that we invite them to our church services whenever they indicate an interest. It's part of our hospitality model and many lives have been changed as a result.

Consider this story: A well-dressed woman arrived at the Portland Airport and immediately hurried outside to hail a taxi. It was a warm summer afternoon a few years back and the vibrant colors of the Pacific Northwest were warm and inviting, yet the turmoil in her heart was as cold as winter. Life had taken its toll on this woman and she wondered if she would live to see another day. Guilt consumed her. Fear kept her trapped inside the prison of her soul.

A cab pulled up and the woman nervously got in. The cab driver noticed immediately that his new passenger seemed apprehensive. When he asked where she wanted to go she said vaguely, "I've arrived here and I don't even have a hotel room." Within moments she was admitting to him that her life was a mess and she didn't know where to turn.

"I know just the place for you," said the driver, "this hotel is a real place of rest," and he drove her to our hotel two miles away from the airport.

David, the children's pastor of Eastside Foursquare Church, was working the front desk of our hotel when the woman checked in. He sensed her agitation and felt compelled to tell her that she was in a safe place and that God loved her. She was stunned. She had never expected to hear words like those at a hotel front desk. David explained in a few words why our hotel existed. Then he told her, "If you need to talk to someone, all you need to do is press "0" on the phone and we'll send pastors to your room."

Within minutes, she was in her room pouring out her heart to two of our female pastors. She admitted that she had come to Portland for a rendezvous with a "lover," and that her husband and children knew nothing of her secret life. She said she used to attend church, but now felt so far away from God that she wasn't sure He would ever take her back.

The compassion and wisdom of our pastors were such a relief to her that she decided to turn her life around. She called her "lover" and told him that she had decided to break off the relationship. Early the next morning, she flew home for a reunion with her family, carrying a new knowledge of the goodness of God, sparked by strangers in a hotel who cared.

Experiences such as those not only change the lives of the people we serve but also forge unity among our staff and develop our love for one another as we work together in this family ministry center. We do the tough jobs together for the sake of the people we serve. We may not always get it right, but we try hard to form genuine relationships with the people that God's sends our way. Our "family ministry center" (FMC) hotel works because the people of Eastside have a servant mentality. Everything flows from a place of service. We don't look down on anyone—staff or hotel guests—we only seek to serve one another.

Nothing in the ordinary standards of the hotel industry requires us to minister to the needs of people at the level we do, but we have chosen an extraordinary path. We recognize that everyone is in some way run down and in need of repair. Even travelers need people in their lives to help them, so we make ourselves available to them without ever imposing ourselves on our hotel guests.

When someone comes to us with a seemingly unsolvable problem, we try to offer practical assistance and encouragement and if they need more help we provide pastoral support and prayer. We never dominate them. We relate to them on the same common ground, like a friend in need. Jesus' disciples are called to be an example of Jesus Himself. That is what we try to do here. We are willing to serve because that is the example of Christ. It's not all about us. It has to be about others.

Employment at a family ministry center is more than a job. It is a relationship. When people work for us, they join our family. We not only train them, we also disciple them. We expect to help people grow when they work for us. They have the opportunity to mature under the mentorship of leaders. That is a tremendous advantage to our guests who know that those who serve them are under authority and learning every day how to serve people even better. Our employees have a mission that is larger than a job and they are passionate about what they do.

Because we are a church operating a mission station for the benefit of travelers and the people in our community, lives are being changed every day at our hotels. Running a hotel that is also a family ministry center like ours is not the only answer to changing the world. Maybe it's not the whole solution to transforming a city, but it's a start. When you think of Jesus' words from Matthew 25, how many other places have the same opportunity as an FMC hotel to fulfill so many of His service requirements simultaneously?

I was hungry and you fed me.
I was thirsty and you gave me a drink.
I was a stranger and you invited me into your home.
I was sick and you cared for me. [2]

In the course of time, people from many geographical locations find their way through our doors and some come to know God. Their testimony of transformation touches others and all of a sudden you can't find a space big enough to hold all of the people seeking change. They think they are checking into a hotel and in the process they discover God. Then they get on an airplane and take that experience with them to other parts of the world.

In many surveys where people rate the greatest influences on their lives, pastors and churches come in somewhere near the bottom. One of the biggest reasons for this phenomenon is that we don't reach out with excellence. We don't go to the places and interact where most people live their lives. We have not provided services that people will pay for in places where they can interact with us and be real. Much of what we call

We need to open our eyes and enlarge our hearts so that we can provide something more for a population in need.

"church" is preaching to people who already know God and sit politely in the seats listening. That is not enough. We need to open our eyes and enlarge our hearts so that we can provide something more for a population in need.

THE SPECIFICS OF EXCELLENCE

Think about how you made a decision on the last hotel where you stayed. Maybe you looked for a favorite hotel chain or maybe you went to Expedia, bitz or Travelocity to find out who had the best rates. Chances are you chose a hotel based on its excellence.

That is what we consistently strive for at Eastside. Every week I look into the faces of people on staff who have become heroes to me because they believe they can make a difference in the world. They sacrifice to see the Kingdom of God expand. They are fulfilling the mission of Eastside—"Building people to touch their world so others will become fully devoted followers of Christ."

Here are three important ways that we consistently bless our customers. Let this be your guide as you infuse excellence into your MBE venture.

1. Treat every guest as you would treat Christ.

This means that no matter who the person is—a guest in the hotel, a customer in the coffee shop, a hurting person in one of our ministries or an individual walking through the door of the church—every person should be treated like Christ, with the utmost decorum, courtesy, warmth and respect.

2. Keep everything new.

It's not enough just to have clean facilities. They must be maintained in a new condition. People like to go to places that are new. New businesses do better than old, outdated businesses. People like new homes, new furniture and new cars. When the carpet is worn out, don't just clean it. Replace it!

3. Treat all people with respect.

Every business needs to think in terms of excellence and in a church-owned business that includes the concept of blessing our guests in everything we do. We are accountable to God as well as our guests, so we do our best to meet or exceed all standards. It isn't about perfection. We will never be perfect, but we can keep doing things better.

People everywhere are looking for someone to believe in them, speak kindly to them and treat them with respect. The Bible says,

"The tongue has the power of life and death."[3] The staff of an FMC hotel recognizes how much people need a few words of encouragement on their solo voyage around the world. Many more people would walk through the door of God's blessing if there were just a few more of us to welcome them and cheer them on. Our commitment to treat others with dignity is one of the reasons that travelers remember us. In order to do that, we try to keep it simple instead of getting weighed down with complicated values and mission statements that we can't live out.

Let's look at a few ways respect can be fostered in an MBE environment:

◆ Scripture is our guide. We will not violate moral and ethical codes of conduct within our hotels or business relationships.

◆ Service is consistently prompt, responsive and delivered when a guest requests something. We assist one other, stepping out of our primary duties when necessary to effectively provide service.

◆ Sincerity with guests shows them we serve them from the heart. We are caring and genuine people who love God. We deliver service with enthusiasm and warmth.

◆ Responsibility for identifying and correcting defects (mistakes, variations, waste and inefficiencies) is everyone's job. If a guest complains to you, you are responsible to initiate the problem-resolution process.

◆ Appearance of our staff is always neat and clean. When we take pride in our appearance, it reflects who we are inside.

◆ Environment is friendly and peaceful. We speak positively about our campus, both within and away from the workplace. Everyone is responsible for creating a great environment that fosters the Spirit of God.

◆ Greeting guests whenever they are within 10 feet of us is one way we make them feel significant. When we stop what we are doing and give them a smile and offer assistance—something they remember because it stands out.

◆ Enthusiasm characterizes our everyday attitudes. We are excited about what God is doing here. We recommend our great services and facilities to the guests.

◆ Respect is consistently obvious in how we treat our guests. We are respectful of our guests' privacy and personal time.

YOUR CALL, TODAY

Have you made this commitment to excellence in your organization? Excellence leads to influence and this is the ultimate business we are in as we aim to help change people's lives for the better.

I want to leave you with one of my favorite verses from Colossians 3:23-24. "Whatever you do, work at it with all your heart, as working for the Lord, not for men, since you know that you will receive an inheritance from the Lord as a reward. It is the Lord Christ you are serving."

This is the ultimate reason for excellence: our work reflects our heart attitude toward God. This is our call as MBEs.

SUMMARY

✚ Excellence is the one vital component behind all successful MBE ventures.

✚ Excellence leads to influence—and that's the real business all MBEs are in—influencing people's lives for good.

✚ Three specific components of excellence in an MBE venture are as follows:

1. Treat every guest as you would treat Christ.

2. Keep everything new. It's not enough just to have clean facilities. They must be maintained in a new condition.

3. Treat all people with respect, no matter what their position, title, job or appearance.

CHAPTER NINE

WHAT A DREAM CAN DO

There were a ton of benefits that the hotel provided for our church in the beginning including a place to meet rent-free, payment of utilities, employment generation and space for ministries. Then, as the hotel's debt has been reduced, we have been blessed with the ability to contribute to other ministries. As our hotels' costs continue to go down, we have more income that we can give toward other areas of need.

This benefit is a huge part of the message of this book—that when your MBE venture is up and running smoothly, the income generated will allow you to branch out in new ways. Your dreams won't be limited by your income.

We've come a long way from when we first rented a building in northeast Portland. Since merging a hotel with our church, our funding has become sustainable and growing. Let's take a look at some of the ways we've been able to branch out. The following are only some of the extended ministries of Eastside:

CHURCH "SERVICES" 24/7

Because we operate a hotel, we can be a 24/7 church that is always open. Our doors never close. If a crisis arises at the hotel, a pastor is on call—male or female. If a guest wants a place to pray, there is a place on site. If a guest needs to talk to a friend, he or she can almost always find one in the coffee shop. Churches that reach out through ministries and church-owned businesses like FMC hotels become more than nice places where people meet for a couple of hours weekly and then the lights are turned off and the doors are locked. With the right vehicles, you can release your God-given, world-changing message to the world 24 hours a day, 7 days a week and have the impact that God desires.

At our hotels (we actually own and run two hotels on one site now), we never aim to preach to people who are unwilling to hear. Our faith flows naturally through our relationship of serving God and our guests. And this happens in a lot of ways. We have a strong value that "belonging comes before believing." Many feel a sense of belonging from the time they check in at the front desk. It is hard to say when they start to believe. Hotel guests may come for only a night and then move on, but some of them are now moving on with God. If travelers want to attend a church service where strangers are made to feel like family, they need go no further than the hotel conference center. We make our church services available to guests in a low-key way. Almost every time we meet for a service, hotel guests join us. Sometimes we know who they are, but often we don't. Each week during those services we invite people to start a relationship with Christ. We record those numbers—an average of one new Christian every three or four days. Many more that we may never see come to Christ on the campus.

ROOM BIBLES

It's a very simple ministry, but it yields big results; we place Bibles in our hotel rooms. The Bibles come with hand-written invitations to take home the Bibles, free for the taking. We go through a lot of Bibles this way.

One day a woman walked into the coffee shop. "Because of this," she said, "my husband is reading the Bible for the first time in his life."

I can see that acorn seed that I picked up in the parking lot of the church on NE Glisan years ago before we moved to this hotel steadily growing. The vision of God is expanding. We can't stop now. We have just begun.

COMMUNITY OUTREACH PROGRAMS

Every year the Eastside Foursquare Church and the Quality Inn & Suites host a "Summer Bash" on our hotel. We team up with Portland radio station 104.1 ("The FISH") and City Team Ministries, a non-profit organization serving the poor and homeless in several metropolitan areas in 38 countries around the world.

On a hot day in July, we invite the community to join us for great music, swimming in the hotel pool, free food and fun with the FISH. We also ask neighbors to bring food items for a homeless shelter in the community and we are able to collect thousands of pounds of food each year. Our hotel guests are invited to participate and some do—even if they just sit on the walkway and watch the crowds. It's a day alive with excitement.

At Eastside, we never close our doors. A community-impact Church lives inside of us. Wherever we go, we carry the Church. We create environments where people can find God in places they already frequent. When you look across America, churches are dying. Denominational numbers are dwindling. Parishes are closing their doors forever. Even churches that record growth may boost their attendance from people hopping over from other churches rather than newcomers entering the doors. People desert the Church when it loses power—when the Light of the World is turned off—but they are attracted to people with passion. People thrive on excitement. They can spot a lifeless entity a mile away, but they can also be energized with enthusiasm when they get involved in something that touches lives and serves those in need.

> People desert the Church when it loses power—when the Light of the World is turned off—but they are attracted to people with passion.

FREEDOM HOUSE

God has called the Church to bring monumental solutions for our community's problems. Every church is making at least a small difference in the people who attend, but what about a world-changing difference? When we bought the hotel, we jumped off a cliff by faith because we believed in the hope that we could change the world. It was a terrifying leap. Great people were advising us, but the final decision to jump was mine. After that first jump, I learned how to get better at cliff-jumping. I knew the journey down. That was what helped me to make one of the most important decisions affecting the future of our family ministry center.

In January 2006, about a year after our church began having services at the hotel, I met a pastor who would bring a revolution to a special group of people in our ministry. About a block away from the hotel, I sat down for lunch with the Rev. Jim Cottrell and a few of his friends at a local restaurant. Before I met Jim, he had worked for 17 years to build Teen Challenge of Portland into a 70-bed facility for men and women with addictions. The Assemblies of God denomination had decided to take over the work just two or three weeks earlier, leaving Jim with a passion to change lives but nowhere to apply it. He needed a place to start a new recovery center.

When you're a mission-based entrepreneur, you often go by gut instincts. You recognize when there is a divine connection and you seize the moment before it passes by forever.

As the MBE of an FMC hotel, I was in a unique position to partner with someone who was able to disciple men who desperately needed help and at the same time could train them to provide services that we needed to maintain the hotel grounds.

Jim and I looked at one another and said, "Let's jump." It barely took us an hour to make the decision to start a residential recovery program called Freedom House on the campus of our family ministry center hotel.

Actually, it was a no-brainer. I was pastoring a community-impact church that was attracting people with addiction problems.

He could provide a one-year recovery program and had a long track record of discipleship and transformed lives. At the same time we could give the men productive work at our hotel. They wouldn't miss work or have to go looking to find work because they lived and worked together with accountability partners right on our property.

The hotel provides Freedom House with 14 rooms in our ministry section and Jim runs his own program. The men learn how to live again by becoming accountable to leadership, one another and God. They keep the hotel looking new by performing vital tasks. They come to church together every Wednesday and Sunday and are a credit to their organization.

These men have made huge sacrifices in their lives for their own transformation. Their passion to change is evident. People in the congregation applaud and support them and make them feel loved and significant, which provides a totally different environment from the drug culture where they came from.

I don't try to control Jim or Freedom House and he doesn't tell me how to run the church. We are co-laborers. We don't always agree but we work things out. He's the expert at what he does. It's a wonderful marriage of the parachurch and the local church. We have successfully graduated men from the program and many more are in training. As soon as possible, Jim and I would like to start Freedom Houses all across the nation. It's a partnership that meets the practical needs of a faith-based hotel business and at the same time rescues people from drug addiction, alcoholism, gangs, pornography and street life. They are never the same again.

Our hotel configuration looks a bit like a fortress. It has L-shaped buildings surrounding inner courtyards with beautiful flowers, a swimming pool and landscaped parking. It has three entrances and exits. That layout reminds me of the protection that God gives us from outside influences while still allowing us to be part of the community. The men in Freedom House are so radically changed that they help us out just like Jeff, our assistant general manager, does. They recognize anyone who comes on the campus with ulterior motives, such as drug-dealers or other criminals and make sure they leave.

Jim is a hero in my book. I understand him because he is another MBE. Along with his wife, Geri, and their five children, they already bought into the vision of transformation, so they joined their vision to ours. Jim comes from a background like the people he now over-sees—living on the streets of Hollywood, sleeping on the floor and running from the law.

One night during a drug deal, a street preacher confronted Jim with the Gospel and he ended up in a "hippie church." He said he heard a message that convinced him that "Jesus Christ alone is the one who understood all my hurt." He said, "I really felt the horrible weight of sin and loneliness lift off my soul and I knew that I was set free from the bondage to drug use, sexual pursuits and street life." The same solution that changed his life he now offers unselfishly to others.

HOMELESS SHELTER

A few years ago, a couple with a passion for providing for the homeless, Dan and Cathe Wiese, became part of our church's pastoral staff. They were running a shelter for the homeless called My Father's House in a duplex that housed five families. They had so many requests that they had to turn away an average of 112 families every month. Cathe educated me on the facts of homelessness. She said more than 3,000 families are homeless on any given night in Multnomah County and the rate of homelessness is growing fast at a rate of 37 percent each year.

When I first met Dan and Cathe, I saw a couple who, like Rita and me, had a dream that they were willing to do something about. Cathe is an MBE with a heart of amazing compassion. She is a true leader and understands the complexities of homelessness like few others. She invited me to become involved. I said yes. Few ever say no to Cathe.

My Father's House is a separate 501(c)(3) organization with its own Board of Directors. While I serve as president and our church members support it financially, Cathe has been the driving force behind this incredible ministry. Too many churches try to duplicate something that is already being done well. It is much better to work together to support those already serving.

In November 2008, My Father's House opened its doors to something that advocates for the homeless could only dream about. It is a brand new, three-story building with 30 individual family apartments. Most public homeless shelters are a desperate attempt to get people off the streets and under a roof, even if people sleep on cots or on the floor. However, many of the homeless are children who are placed at great risk from predators in those environments.

The average age of a homeless person in our community is nine years old. We see more homeless families than homeless singles and we have seen more than a 50 percent increase in single fathers among the homeless just in the past year. The father keeps his children with him as he roams the streets without a job.

When we started, we didn't realize the new My Father's House would eventually become a 27,000 square foot, $3.9 million building project and the largest facility of its kind without government support in the United States. The complex is located a few miles away from our church/hotel. God gave us success after success. My Father's House does not accept any state or federal funding. Instead, 140 churches from diverse denominational backgrounds joined together with community leaders and businessmen to help raise the needed funds. Cathe wrote grant proposals and received money from foundations like the Bill and Melinda Gates Foundation, M. J. Murdock Charitable Trust and Mission Increase Foundation, just to name a few.

Each unit in the complex provides a safe place for a family to gather itself together and start a new life. Each one has an outside lock on the door with a key entry like a hotel, individual heat and air conditioning control, a private bathroom with new towels and shower curtain for each new family and an equipped kitchenette with cabinets, a small refrigerator and a microwave.

The hotel-like environment of the complex not only speaks of welcome to guests but also gives them a sense of dignity and significance—two characteristics that homeless people desperately need for future success. The atmosphere is also a breath of fresh air for volunteers. It generates a feeling of excitement that makes them want to come back. As a result, the shelter has attracted 300 volunteers, a remarkable number. Some volunteers equip entire rooms with furniture or provide sets of towels and dishes for each new family.

Most of the people who come to live at My Father's House have been beaten up by life. Many have been abused from the time they were children. Usually they have been homeless for a few weeks or months and we are usually not the first place where they have looked for shelter. They may have stayed with friends and family and sometimes were kicked out because they lost a job, separated or perhaps had bad behavior. At other times they had to leave because of landlords or tenant laws. Maybe they wore out their welcome or got into arguments and were forced to leave.

If they spent time in another homeless shelter, it might have been uncomfortable and maybe even unsafe. When they come to us, it may be the first time in months or even years that they had a room to call their own. It seems like a taste of heaven to them.

The predominant reason the people in our shelter are homeless is financial. We love them like parents who want their children to succeed and come of age. We help them look for work and find a permanent place to live. We have a great success rate in transformed lives.

GARBAGE DUMP CHURCH PLANT

A courageous couple that led Eastside's first church plant took a seemingly impossible risk that few other people would have taken, because they heard God cheering them on. Ramon Baca and his wife, Miriam, launched an outreach to 1,500 sickly, malnourished Nicaraguan children and adults who live in La Chureca, the Managua city dump.

Yes, the city dump.

Every day dump residents claw their way through smoking piles of stinking garbage, gasping for breath, trying to find something to sell to buy food for their families. Parents sell their little girls—some as young as eight years old—as prostitutes for the dump truck drivers. Sexually transmitted diseases and other infections are rampant.

Ramon and Miriam call their church in the dump "The Lighthouse" because they carry the light of hope in the midst of darkness and despair. They didn't start this church outside the dump. They started it *inside* the dump. That's edgy.

At their first worship service, 230 people attended and 18 began a new relationship with Christ. They now have three weekly home groups. In one group, three couples decided to be married. They say they are "pushing back the darkness and shining the bright light of Christ in that neighborhood."

MINISTRIES THAT MATCH THE TIMES

As Christians, we have a relationship with the One who created the world. He has given us His inheritance of world ownership. When we put our faith into action, people come to us. When they are not coming, that means we need to develop new models in step with the times to deliver the Christian message.

Transformation is the nature of the true Gospel. It transforms everything. It is revolutionary and forever alters the path of those who step through its door. The good news of the Gospel says that whatever is broken can be fixed, including people. When the true Light of the world comes, the change is measurable. We don't need to manufacture it or hype it up. People will see it.

We describe the partnership between family ministry centers, churches and businesses as a triangle with these main points:

◆ **Prayer.** The inner core is prayer. It's what centers everything and is the fuel that sparks every dream.

◆ **Church.** At the top are the typical church functions such as church services, Bible study, youth and children's ministries, etc.

◆ **Social Service.** For us, social service is taking care of the poor and needy. For Christ, it was not optional to act on the principles of love and justice. Scripture is filled with instructions outlining our responsibilities to the widows, orphans and the poor. The prophet Isaiah said it this way: "If you spend yourselves in behalf of the hungry and satisfy the needs of the oppressed, then your light will rise in the darkness and your night will become like the noonday."[1]

◆ **Business.** The final component is business. Most churches have the core of prayer and then only one point of the triangle—church functions. A few churches add a second point—social service. We have added the third component—business—to answer the problem of sustainability.

Desperate times call for desperate measures. Faced with life and death situations in the world, Christians have no alternative. Either we change the world or the world loses the battle. It's our call. People should be beating down our doors to hear the message of hope. When they are not, perhaps we can offer a service that they will pay for—such as hospitality—or meet a need in the community that they can understand—like homelessness. Then they will be exposed to an expression of the Gospel that they can understand one that can change their lives.

The three-point model of church, social service and business—with an inner soul of prayer—creates a sustainable model that can last into the future and have a measurable impact on any community. In order for the Church to survive financially as a transforming force in society, something has to start changing in our way of thinking.

Change requires fresh ideas—shifting the paradigm back to the biblical foundation.

The early Church operated within society. Its leaders were business people (fishermen, tax collectors, land owners, tent makers) and were present in the marketplace on a daily basis. The book of Acts records how they, "devoted themselves to the apostles' teaching and to the fellowship, to the breaking of bread and to prayer. Everyone was filled with awe and many wonders and miraculous signs were done by the apostles. All the believers were together and had everything in common. Selling their possessions and goods, they gave to anyone as he had need. Every day they continued to meet together in the temple courts. They broke bread in their homes and ate together with glad and sincere hearts, praising God and enjoying the favor of all the people. And the Lord added to their number daily those who were being saved."[2]

The first church meeting place was somebody's house. It was a place within the community that people already frequented. It was a place of hospitality, filled with people poised to change the world. They met house to house, neighborhood to neighborhood, taking the Church with them wherever they went. Two thousand years later, Eastside is here as testimony of their efforts.

HOW ABOUT YOU?

Want other ideas for reaching people outside of your church or non-profit? Instead of a fellowship hall, envision a conference and performing arts center where people want to come every day, whether or not they're part of your ministry.

Or consider how many hours people spend at the gym each week. At your family ministry center you can add a gym with a basketball court and a fitness center that nearby residents can use as well as hotel guests. Add a smoothie stand or fast-food health bar. Give people a reason to stick around for some old-fashioned hospitality. Maybe even loop last week's sermon video on one of the TV monitors.

When the neighborhood declines and local people can no longer pay to maintain the church through donations, does the church sell its property for a profit and move away or does God have more creative solutions for us today?

Your dreams aren't limited anymore. With business as the important third axis of your triangle, your venture will be able to have the sustainable and increased funding it needs to look to the future. What will you be able to do now?

SUMMARY

+ Once your MBE venture begins to bring in consistent income and your mission is funded sustainably, you will want to look to expansion, future opportunities or additional ways your mission can be implemented.

+ At Eastside, we've funded a counseling center, recovery ministry, homeless shelter and planted a church internationally—in a garbage dump.

+ Think of the partnership between family ministry centers, churches and businesses as a triangle where prayer is the inner core, then church, business and social services are all integral components within the larger triangle.

+ Once sustainable and discretionary income begins to consistently be generated, your organization's dreams aren't limited anymore. With business as the important third axis of your triangle, your venture will be able to have the sustainable and increased funding it needs to look to the future. What will you be able to do now?

CHAPTER TEN

HOTELS AND MORE

About a year ago I was in Washington, DC, speaking to a group of pastors and leaders about the changes we have seen in Portland because of the Christian hospitality model of Eastside Foursquare Church. After I finished, I was introduced to an African-American bishop who is the influential leader of an established church in the area—he's an amazing transformational leader.

"Eric, my current church campus covers almost a full city block," the bishop said. "This city isn't the kind of place that has much land available. It's built up. All of the plots are taken, so our church sits on a prime piece of real estate. We've had several strong offers to sell. One was from a national hotel chain. They're looking to buy us out, tear down our church buildings and put up a high-rise hotel. Honestly, Eric, we're thinking about taking the offer and moving to the suburbs."

They already bought 120 acres in the suburbs and could easily have left. I couldn't really blame him. When he told me the amount of the offer, I felt like letting out a low whistle. The amount was several times what we had paid for our hotel. (Then again, this was the nation's capital, with some of the highest property values on the East Coast.) There was no doubt that they could sell high, pocket the multi-million-dollar payment and move out of the city. With the money from the sale, the church could build a brand-new, state-of-the-art church facility with all the trimmings.

But although the plan looked good on paper, something was slowing him down. He knew there was more to consider here than building a big new church building. They had run into a few road-blocks concerning their suburban property that had kept them from making the move. "Listening to you talk just now," the bishop said, "I started wondering if maybe I don't have to move away from our location after all. Maybe we could build a hotel of our own and stay downtown."

I smiled. "Let's go have coffee and talk," I said. "I've got some ideas I'd like to run by you."

The bishop was not one to abandon local people if he thought they needed him. If the church left its current location, it would amount to an uncharacteristic retreat. He is a world-changer who has planted more than 70 churches. This church has been in the city for many years and has established a prominent position of community influence. He sensed that he still had work to do there.

After that meeting, we entered a hotel partnership with this bishop through the Christian Asset Network (CAN) that will be a tremendous advantage to his church and also a benefit to his city. He's not moving out. He's transforming his current ministry and incorporating a sustainable funding model that will be able to propel his ministry into the next level of success.

In this chapter we'll take a look at doing exactly that. You may be facing a decision to sell all and move to the suburbs, whatever your "suburbs" may be. But there is another alternative and that's to move into an MBE position with your current venture and see if there's a way to leverage what you currently have to move into your next sphere of calling.

HOTELS AND MORE

As you may recall from a few chapters back, Torre Morgal and I created CAN to provide a way for churches and ministries to enter the hospitality business without prior experience. CAN is a professional services company with long experience in the hotel industry. When leaders partner with CAN, the people behind them not only know the market but also provide access to strategic partnerships for the leaders' success. You will find more information in the Appendix and on our website, www.KingdomPoint.com.

Specifically to the bishop's situation, CAN developed a plan that will allow the church to stay on their land. They will prosper financially on a long-term basis through ownership. Instead of receiving a one-time purchase price for the sale of the church and land, they have now set up an ongoing revenue stream that will continue to increase for the foreseeable future and also drive traffic to their church. New people will flood onto the property on a daily basis to use the hotel and conference center and they will have an opportunity to touch many lives.

As a first step, the bishop and his leaders decided to turn down all offers for their property. They stood their ground and the church stepped through the doors on the deal to build a multi-million-dollar, ultra-modern hotel and conference center on their site. Like Eastside, they will now hold services in the conference facility while offering Christian hospitality through the hotel. CAN will help them develop their dream.

This partnership between the bishop's church and CAN is proving to be a giant leap forward in that church's outreach to their city. Their city block will receive a much-needed facelift. Instead of continuing to use their old, worn-out church building, they will tear it down and erect a sparkling, glass-enclosed conference center that will also be the meeting place for their congregation. The city is backing them and so is a significant hotel chain. The new hotel and conference center are poised to bring new business to the city, generating revenue and bringing outsiders into the community. Plus (the importance of this cannot be understated) the city government will now receive tax revenues from the hotel.

> Because of CAN, pastors and Christian leaders are able to have mentors and more as they pursue future multi-million-dollar hotel projects.

Because of CAN, pastors and Christian leaders are able to have mentors and more as they pursue future multi-million-dollar hotel projects. Whenever a ministry demonstrates an interest in starting a Christian hospitality business, CAN is in place to show them how to start the journey and succeed along the way. CAN has set the standard to solve the complex problems of combining business and ministry. We can help boost performance and at the same time maximize the value of operations for the benefit of investors. Through our hands-on approach, we work with a ministry to develop a uniquely Christian strategy that equals and exceeds the standards of other hotels. We help to improve the operation and increase the value of the hotel investment while at the same time carrying out a vision for ministry.

CAN helps pastors and Christian leaders understand the unique perspective and maintain the spiritual balance required by churches and ministries. Because of CAN, MBEs will not have to learn the hospitality business from scratch all by themselves. First, we educate leaders as Christian hoteliers with the idea that they will run their own hotels themselves soon. Later, they can teach others what they have learned and become a part of the vision to launch 350 hospitality models within the next fifteen years. In business we call it franchising. In the Church we call it discipleship.

In the near future we hope to invite 12 high level leaders at a time to Portland to learn this model. We'll disciple them while they live on-site at our campus at Eastside. They'll attend classes, work in the hotel and learn how we coordinate the business with the church and ministries like Freedom House. This model is based on the idea of biblical multiplication. New MBEs will be created who will build new organizations that will help transform communities, generate financial success and continue to spread the model. If you're interested in being one of these leaders, please e-mail me (contact information is provided in the Appendix) and we'll add your name to our database so that when this program is established you'll be the first to know.

You may not wish to partner with CAN. That's perfectly okay. I encourage you to find the partner(s) who will help you in your venture. I learned early on that I needed a good businessman such as Torre to stand with me if I ever wanted to learn and succeed in the hospitality business. Without his help, advice and vision we wouldn't be here today. I knew that what he had done for me we needed to do for others. That was why we started CAN.

In December 2003, shortly after I went to work for Torre and while I was working bi-vocationally at our church plant, we closed our first hotel deal. I was the primary leader in negotiations for a $3.7 million project. Believe me, I was nervous. I was constantly on the phone with Torre and Bob Burkette, our hotel broker, asking, "What do I do next?" But with their mentorship, I was able to put the deal together and four years later the property was worth $7.5 million. Torre introduced me to other great business people and mentors like Bob, who helped us acquire our current family ministry center hotel and never accepted payment. Bob has always told me that a deal is nothing more than the "engineering of consent." He has been in the hotel business most of his life. Bob was tough on me, but I learned quickly that he was often right.

There is no way we could have succeeded with Eastside Foursquare Church's business ventures without the help of great attorneys, accountants, brokers and partners. I had so much to learn and people like Bob and Torre along with the partners of Lincoln Asset Management have always stood with me to make something happen for the Kingdom. They have celebrated successes along the way and have brainstormed with me in the challenges of the hospitality industry, which you know by now I see as a natural fit for churches.

KINGS AND PRIESTS

I point leaders toward the hospitality industry as a natural merger of the biblical roles of kings and priests who operate Kingdom businesses. There are other models for business and we'll talk about them shortly. But let me first just cast a vision for merging your non-profit with a hotel and let me explain what I mean by the merger of kings and priests.

When I first met Torre, we were up in Kelowna, British Columbia, attending a denominational youth function. I was still living in Woodinville at the time. When I heard Torre talk about the hospitality business, I was intrigued. We talked for hours, long into the night, debating the pros and cons of churches that developed business models and what it would look like for a church to own a hotel. That discussion led us into a consideration of the contrasting biblical roles of kings and priests.

The role of a priest is the ministry side of an MBE venture. In biblical history, kings provided the resources for the building of the sanctuary while the priests provided communication with God. The priests knew and communicated God's will and the kings provided the resources to accomplish it. The role of priests includes both communication with God in prayer and the implementing of those prayers in developing ministry objectives that serve others' needs.

> In biblical history, kings provided the resources for the building of the sanctuary while the priests provided communication with God.

As mentioned, the first priority for a ministry before entering a business venture is to clearly define its mission objectives. First you clarify your mission, then you clarify your vehicle. Mission always precedes money. If you put money first and expect to get around to planning your mission later, it won't work. Your mission must be clear before you establish your business entity in the total picture. Originally, Torre felt that the hotel and church had to be kept separate. He pointed out many potential problems with the merger and his insight helped me refine the vision. Eventually, as we worked through the details together, we were both convinced that this was a sovereign move that God was doing—an entrepreneurial basis for the transformation of cities by the merger of churches and Kingdom businesses.

The role of a king is the business side of the venture. Like many pastors, I distrusted the business world and its focus on what seemed to me the unspiritual realm of profit-making. But Torre prevailed. We came to a meeting of the minds. I don't keep them separate any longer. We are in business but we are also advancing the Kingdom.

Torre has told me many times that most ministry people have wrong thinking about money. The first book he gave me was *Rich Dad Poor Dad* by Robert Kiyosaki and Sharon Lechter. Then he gave me more resources to develop my thinking. He said, "The only difference between people who have money and those who don't is their thinking." I was the pastor but he said I was the one who had to be transformed by the renewing of my mind![1]

CAN merges the king and priest roles to make a significant impact for the Church in the business community. The primary purpose for everything we do is reaching people with the love of Christ, because we know that Jesus is the answer for the problems of the world. While money is vital to the momentum of ministry, it is even more vital when a hotel guest decides to follow Christ and his teachings. While the money the guest paid for his room supports the work of the Kingdom, it was the Church that provided a life-transforming message. Both are needed.

As we've talked about all through this book, one of the greatest limitation churches face in touching people's lives is funding. As I have said several times throughout this book, it is possible to establish sustainable funding sources biblically. Joseph saved his father and brothers because he had a funding source—the harvests of Egypt. A church owning and operating a hotel has a self-sustaining funding source. As Christian hotel ownership increases, other related businesses will emerge to provide goods and services that meet the criteria for both ministry and business. These ventures will provide opportunities for business partnerships between churches, ministries, developers and investors.

Under this umbrella, a hotel can become more than a place for lodging guests. It can serve as the location for housing other businesses alongside the church that meets in the conference center. These mixed-use developments can be located in both urban and resort settings in high profile hospitality properties that present a picture of a church that prospers both spiritually and naturally.

I believe the Christian hospitality industry is a natural fit for Christian entrepreneurs willing to create products and services to meet the needs of this emerging industry. For example, they can provide Internet service that blocks pornography or television channels that are safe for children or a long list of products that are needed in a family ministry center hotel. The church becomes stronger when business and ministry collaborate and their partnerships are backed by biblical principles. Then, instead of the church driving away businesses and entrepreneurs, you rent them office space in your hotel. When the church is not holding meetings, the auditorium becomes a for-profit meeting space that can be rented out to the public.

> When I equip people with an entrepreneurial vision, I light fires. How many fires can I start?

The Bible says that it is my job to equip God's people for works of service.[2] When I equip people with an entrepreneurial vision, I light fires. How many fires can I start? If I light you on fire, the Kingdom of God is expanded. If you start burning, the person standing next to you catches fire. The movement becomes a forest fire spreading the vision around the world.

Those who attend churches pastored by people of character who are also prosperous in business will begin to catch the fire. The members will have a model of both provision for their families and wealth they can give away, just like their leader. They will become unified by a common concern for others and an appreciation of God's faithfulness in bountifully supplying all their needs. That is how you create revival. That is how you create a movement.

The church right now needs not only a spiritual revival but also a revival of wealth like the patriarchs of the past. Put simply, we need more Christian millionaires who function in MBE roles. We have been rich in faith but now we need to be rich in goods to carry out our faith. Especially in times of economic crisis, the Church needs to prosper, because that gives evidence to the world that true prosperity comes from God. We are not limited by economic conditions.

OTHER VEHICLES

It may not be feasible in your mission to merge with a hotel funding vehicle. That's okay. When the main pieces of the formula are in place, the right funding vehicle will come together. Other funding vehicles might include malls, restaurants and cafes, bookstores and insurance companies. Whatever works for your mission.

A few examples of this in action:

◆ In the mid-1990s, Kirbyjon Caldwell, a Wharton MBA who sold bonds for First Boston before he enrolled in seminary, formed an economic development corporation that revived a depressed neighborhood near Houston's 14,000-member Windsor Village United Methodist Church, which he now heads.

◆ Today, a former Kmart now houses a mix of church and private businesses employing 270 people, including a Christian school and a bank. New plans call for a massive center with senior housing, retailing and a public school. See their website at http://www.kingdombuilders.com

◆ Another example is Ebenezers, a first class, fully operational coffeehouse that seeks to serve the community of Capitol Hill in Washington, DC. Their motto is that they serve "coffee with a cause." The coffee shop is owned and operated by National Community Church and all profits go toward community outreach projects. See their website at: http://ebenezerscoffeehouse.com/

◆ A third example is an MBE styled venture in Florida called Potter's House Ministries. They have successfully merged their church with a mall. See their website at: http://www. potters-house.org/

Their original Potter's House facility was not able to accommodate the growth of the ministry. Knowing this, ministry leaders purchased an abandoned car dealership with the idea to transform it into a new church sanctuary. They began to renovate it while holding services at a different location. A new 800-seat sanctuary, gymnasium/ youth church, recording studio, nursery and classrooms were completed a year later, with a new school completed shortly after that.

Believing that God wanted them to reach the community, the ministry purchased a 41,000 square foot former AT&T phone center and renovated into a multi-purpose facility that housed a multiplicity of businesses (many of which were owned by members), including a federal credit union, dry cleaners, café, law offices, men's clothing, gift shops, Greyhound bus terminal, a beauty salon and barber shop and dance studio.

A few years later, the Potter's House purchased another 48-acre, 376,000 square feet shopping complex formerly known as Normandy Mall. The mall was run down and the ministry revitalized it. In November 2003 a portion of this massive space (the 103,000 square foot Sam's Wholesale Club), was converted to accommodate the need for church growth and the facilitation of additional ministries within the local church. Once the first phase of the new facility was completed, (which included a 4,200 seat sanctuary and an 11,000 square foot nursery) a different facility was converted to accommodate the growth of the school by creating new classrooms and a gymnasium. In 2005 phase two of the mall renovations were completed, which included an 800-seat children's church, a coffee shop and teen café, a full recording studio, a lecture hall, a wedding chapel, conference rooms, administrative offices, book store and much more.

In Spring of 2006 renovations began on the last 177,000 square foot of the mall. Today it's the home of the region's largest shopping venue and now known as Kingdom Plaza. A 300 seat restaurant anchors the mall along with a fitness and aqua center. Anchoring the east end of the mall is a 22 lane bowling alley and game room called King Pins Bowling center. The mall also is the home to a full service day spa, jewelry store, florist, tee shirt shop, pro bowl shop, women's shoe store, cellular phone store, health food store, medical supplies store, insurance company, realty offices, full day care and pre-school center and a barber shop.

How's that for realizing a dream?!

YOUR PLAN TODAY

Is God leading you to begin an MBE venture? There's a hurting world out there who needs the results an MBE venture produces.

Know your mission.

Decide on your funding vehicle.

Develop your partnership network.

And begin.

SUMMARY

✛ Hotels are a perfect funding vehicle for faith-based MBE ventures because they provide an obvious funding solution, attract a variety of people for ministry purposes and lend well to the greater mission of promoting community transformation.

✛ We've developed a specific education and training source called the Christian Asset Network (CAN) to help MBEs succeed in the hotel industry.

✛ It may not be feasible with your specific mission to merge with a hotel funding vehicle. That's okay. When the main pieces of the formula are in place, the right funding vehicle will come together. Other funding vehicles might include storage units, restaurants and cafes, bookstores, malls and insurance companies. Whatever works best for your mission.

THE AGE OF THE EDGY MBE

One Sunday I was up front preaching at Eastside when a guy in the first row jumped to his feet and started frantically patting himself down.

He appeared completely oblivious to his actions. I could see that I was quickly losing everyone's attention. The guy just kept patting and patting. Every eye was soon on him, including mine. I tried to keep talking but my mind was racing to what might come next. Whatever was happening, I hoped the guy would naturally move toward the doors and exit, but he wasn't budging. Finally he found a lighter in one of his pockets and pulled it out, his eyes brightening. Then he started another pat-down search—what good is a lighter when you still need a cigarette? The patting continued uninterrupted for several more minutes. Everyone in the congregation was hopelessly absorbed now, looking curiously back and forth to see how I would handle this. I didn't want to embarrass the guy as a guest, but I knew I couldn't have him lighting up in the middle of the service. "Hey, buddy," I said at last. "You know, in this church it's perfectly okay if you want to take a smoke break. We've got a smoking area right outside the door."

He paused for a moment, then grinned and slurred, "Y'know rev'rund, that would be great." He found his cigarette at last, turned and walked out.

How do you make a smooth segue out of that? The incident struck me as so funny. We were such an atypical church. "You know, I just love this place!" I said and everybody laughed; the comment broke the tension. That was the first time somebody had ever interrupted one of our church services to take a smoke break.

Welcome to the new trend of the edgy MBE venture—the wave of the future and a reminder of the past, when Jesus was the preacher and all kinds of extraordinary people came around Him and He loved them into the Kingdom. Those men and women initially did not know how to act around Christ. The church protocol had not yet been established. Following Christ was raw. It was real. It was revolutionary.

This is the type of leadership I'm inviting you to now. Don't be afraid to lead an edgy venture. When your mission is truly reaching people who need help, you can't help but raise a few eyebrows.

AN EDGY PROSPERITY

If sermons alone could win the world to Christ, it would have already happened. Enough great messages have been preached to win it many times over. Apparently the Church's message hasn't reached enough desperate people through preaching alone because statistics show in some places we are losing the battle. In many communities people no longer walk through the doors of the church and attendance is at all time lows.

> Cities are transformed not by preaching alone but by preaching combined with personal commitment to go out the doors of the church building and into doors of the world.

Cities are transformed not by preaching alone but by preaching combined with personal commitment to go out the doors of the church building and into the doors of the world—getting right inside and then going out to love and serve the people outside for the good of all, regardless of the personal cost to you.

That guy in the front row at Eastside wasn't the only person who was reached that day. The congregation was able to see how we handled the unexpected. They saw an example of a church that welcomes all people. We didn't plan it that way, but because our doors are open to everyone, that kind of unexpected thing is going to happen. Our community-impact church and faith-based hotel business make it possible for us to be there for edgy people. They don't feel as if they are walking through the doors of a traditional church. They feel at home. That's what we want.

Uncommon people tend to drop in on us all the time. Four years ago, shortly after we held our first Easter service at the hotel conference center, a young woman named Ivy saw me on TV and decided to visit the church. Even though she had grown up in a church home, her life had taken a wrong turn. She became a prostitute at the age of 13 and then many years later became the girlfriend of the leader of a white supremacist gang leader, whom I'll call Jerry.

Very soon after coming to Eastside, Ivy found a personal relationship with God and began to fight her way back out of the many impossible situations in her life. The first time she tried to explain to me the change in her life, she could only think of street language to express herself. She said, with all seriousness, "I used to be Jerry's bitch, but now I'm Jesus' bitch."

Her words stunned me. All of my inner sensibilities of what church looked like had crumbled around me. I tried hard not to reflect outwardly the astonishment I felt inwardly. As a pastor, however, I took her words as an unmovable reminder that not only did Ivy need the church, but the church needed Ivy. God was throwing the door wide open to unusual people and ministry possibilities I had never dreamed of.

Since then Ivy has turned her life around in a miraculous way. This past year she was married. She blesses our church with her transformed life and her openness to people. Every week she fills rows of seats with friends who need Christ in their lives. I have seen Jesus in

Ivy and have been so proud of one who has fought hard to change her life. Life beat her down, but Ivy stood up and said yes to a new life with Christ.

When people who are helpless, addicted, or homeless meet Christians who are confidently dependent on God, you have an edgy church. When God stood on the edge before He created the world, there was no model of what earth needed to look like. He simply spoke and a new world came into being. The image of God resides in you and me. God is looking for people who will stand and speak life into people on the edge and tell them of a bright new future of prosperity and hope. He needs people with enough money to not only shout encouragement but also finance the voyage.

People have asked me why we don't move off campus into a larger building; I believe that America has enough large auditoriums away from the kind of people we reach. We need more messy ones where the service seems out of control but actually God is at work reaching people who need Him, using Christians who trust Him and try to do His will. We can't keep moving away from places of need. We must go to those places and stay there, trusting God to turn our land into a promised place of blessing.

Another story: One Sunday a preschool teacher who works in a nearby public school pressed a red coin in my hand that she had earned for ending her heroin habit and staying clean for 30 days. The words on the front of the coin said, "To thine own self be true—1 recovery month."

This beautiful woman with amazing gifts knew she wouldn't shock me. She knew I would cheer her on. When you're severely addicted, it's hard to climb out of that hole. Every time you try, you feel as if the edges of that grave are caving in on you. You need someone to encourage you and fight that battle with you. Maybe you made some bad choices, but your situation isn't hopeless.

I have known people who would shoot heroin before a morning service at our church and then sit in the back row with their hands raised in worship. Prostitutes have turned tricks and come to church the next day. At least they came to church. It is amazing and exciting to me that they keep coming and get changed. How different their lives become when they just don't give up and we don't give up on them, either. We don't shut the door in their faces or drive them away. Often these edgy people just need to hear us say, "I'm so proud of you. You can make it." When they hear those words, their faces light up. It's not the response they anticipated. It gives them hope for a new tomorrow.

Some congregations would never allow a prostitute into their church, but the radical thought here is that in some ways the Church has become a prostitute. Why are some churches so ineffective in their efforts? Why are so many churches suffering from a lack of resources? It's not because God doesn't want them to prosper, as some people would have us believe. The real reason is that the

> Whenever our passion for our First Love has faded, we can only regain our privileged position with God when we walk down the aisle of faith escorted by the Holy Spirit and faithfully pledge ourselves once again to Christ, our Husband.

Church is ineffective and poor when it becomes unfaithful to God. In effect, the Church becomes a prostitute.

Like Gomer in the book of Hosea, the eyes of the Church have wandered to other lovers. The Bible records this description of unfaithfulness, "When the Lord first began speaking to Israel through Hosea, He said to him, 'Go and marry a prostitute, so that some of her children will be conceived in prostitution. This will illustrate how Israel has acted like a prostitute by turning against the Lord and worshiping other gods.'"[1]

Whenever our passion for our First Love has faded, we can only regain our privileged position with God when we walk down the aisle of faith escorted by the Holy Spirit and faithfully pledge ourselves once again to Christ, our Husband.[2]

God wants the Church to see that she has loved substitutes for God more than God Himself. Programs, power, position and lifeless church services can dominate the life of the Church while God waits for us to love Him passionately as a faithful wife loves her Husband. When you love God first, you can handle edgy situations like the drug addict who wanted a smoke and the prostitute who sought after Jesus. You understand their yearning need to know Him and you would never stand in their way.

Whenever we realize what we are doing wrong and return to God, His great blessings await us. Hosea describes this, too. "When she runs after her lovers, she won't be able to catch up with them. She will search for them but not find them. Then she will think, 'I might as well return to my husband because I was better off with him than I am now.'"[3]

God repeatedly tells Israel that times of prosperity will come if they stay faithful to Him. Throughout the Old Testament, He speaks a message of blessing and affluence for His children. He wants to lead His children to a better land, a brighter tomorrow and places of authority and honor—if we will just listen and obey Him.

> The day of Jezreel is a message for today's Church. It comes to pass when a congregation is planted in the land as a representative of God—without apology—and then begins to prosper.

God wants us to take our inheritance as His sons and daughters. God didn't come up with the idea that His children would remain destitute and broke. He says just the opposite. He says He will make us a great nation—"If you listen to these commands of the Lord your God that I am giving you today and if you carefully obey them, the Lord will make you the head and not the tail and you will always be on top and never at the bottom."[4]

The day of Jezreel is another biblical example of this edgy prosperity in action. Jezreel was the name of the firstborn son of Hosea and Gomer. Jezreel represents the people of God who have wandered away from Him and are being once again planted in the land. Jezreel is an image of prosperity. The Bible describes this day like this: "Yet the time will come when Israel will prosper and become a great nation. In that day its people will be like the sands of the seashore—too many to count! Then, at the place where they were told, 'You are not my people,' it will be said, 'You are children of the living God.' Then the people of Judah and Israel will unite under one leader and they will return from exile together. What a day that will be—the day of Jezreel—when God will again plant His people in His land."[5]

The day of Jezreel is a message for today's Church. It comes to pass when a congregation is planted in the land as a representative of God—without apology—and then begins to prosper. Then comes a day of great rejoicing as the Church's prosperity begins to change the city. Yes, there are giants in the land. Problems still exist. Any time you enter your promised land you will find Canaanites, Hittites and Jebusites, but that cannot stop the children of the living God from uniting and returning from exile with great joy.

INVITED TO PROSPER

Across the street from our Sacred Grounds Espresso coffee shop and family ministry center is a cemetery where some of the area's homeless people spend their time. Some days they wander in for a cup of coffee, looking for life and stability in our environment.

The Bible describes the Church as wandering and homeless when she refuses to accept what God has destined for her to receive. Her womb doesn't give birth. Her breasts don't give milk. She is barren and her future is closed up.[6] However, God says He will win back His wandering wife and speak tenderly to her once again.[7] When God sent Hosea to bring back Gomer, it was a picture of God restoring His wandering and homeless bride. It's recorded like this: "Then the Lord said to me, 'Go and get your wife again. Bring her back to you and love her, even though she loves adultery. For the Lord still loves Israel even though the people have turned to other gods, offering them choice gifts.'"[8]

Why don't Christians truly prosper? It's not because God forbids us to have wealth but because we don't use our brains. God says "alcohol and prostitution have robbed my people of their brains."[9] Alcohol and prostitution represent an identity crisis. That is where many Christians find themselves today. They just don't understand that the Church owns it all, as far as the eye can see. This ownership goes clear back to the beginning of time when God made man and placed him in a fruitful garden of prosperity, giving him dominion and authority. The Church only stands "alone and unprotected, like a helpless lamb in an open field"[10] because she is ignorant of who she really is—the Bride of the Lamb.

The Scriptures take us on a journey back to God. He is constantly trying to restore mankind to the place of blessing that He has prepared, but we just don't get it. Some people of the past walked through the open door of blessing—like Daniel and Abraham—but others were content to stand on the other side, fearful of the journey into the unknown. How can the Church find her way back to wealth and influence in our communities? We must realize first that we really do own it all and it has been given to us by Christ Himself.

How does a church, or any faith-based non-profit, get on the path toward true prosperity? The first step is to return to our First Love.[11] The Bible says, "Let us press on to know Him! Then He will respond to us as surely as the arrival of dawn or the coming of rains in early spring."[12] When God says, "I want Israel to be a prosperous vine," that is a picture of great prosperity and fruitfulness. Whenever we return to Him, then He can show us the way through the door of blessing.

Returning to God is an invitation to obedience. That requires action on your part. You have to do something. You must open the door and walk through. I believe that in order for the Church to prosper today we must remain in close relationship with the One who created it all for our enjoyment and be willing to steward it well. Abraham met God and God sent him in the direction of a new land.

Your new land could be ownership of a business that helps other people find God.

SAIL ON!

I once read a story about a young man preparing to leave on a solo voyage around the world in a homemade boat. Almost everyone on the pier was filling him with fear by telling him what could go wrong. They said things such as:

"The sun will broil your skin!"

"Your food won't last!"

"Your boat can't withstand the waves."

"You'll never make it!"

But as the boat drifted out to sea, one person waved his arms and shouted, "Bon Voyage! You can make it! We're proud of you! Sail on!"

Sail on—that one voice of encouragement made all the difference. The young man told people that after he returned from his voyage around the world, safe and sound.

I'm glad that visionaries of the past refused to listen to those dream killers on the pier. Instead, they heard the voice cheering them on. Consider:

Thomas Edison didn't give up on the light bulb, even though his helpers seriously doubted that the thing would work. Every time one experiment failed, he said he was one step closer to finding out what would succeed.

Charles Lindbergh flew across the Atlantic alone, even though everyone he knew told him he was flirting with death.

Papa Ten Boom risked his life and the life of his family to say "Yes" to frightened Jews in Holland who needed a safe refuge in The Hiding Place away from the Nazis.

Julliard School of Music saw beyond the ravages of polio by welcoming in an unlikely violin student on crutches named Itzhak Pearlman.

Our Lord Jesus held nothing back when He left heaven, came to earth and went for it—all the way to the cross and beyond—to show us that we really do own it all through Him.

Are you in a homemade boat, thinking seriously about sailing, except for those dismal voices you hear around you or within? Do you see before you an ocean of possibilities, or do you see the potential of failure and death?

The voices of gloom that keep the Church deprived are not God's voice. God is at the end of the pier, shouting encouragement and cheering us on. Can't you see Him now, standing there, His arms outstretched, waving at you, believing in you, wanting you to be everything He created you to be? He is telling you that you will prosper, regardless of the risks, because He's your Guide. He's your Provider. Your Coach. You can confidently depend on Him.

Martin Luther King, Jr., said, "Faith is taking the first step even when you don't see the whole staircase." It's time to step through the open doorway to the sustainable wealth that God has provided for the Church to truly prosper. Are you standing at the edge of the doorway into your dream, peering into the future? So many people think the door is closed to them, but it's not. Your dream is right around the corner, waiting.

So sail on. You can do it! Sail on!

SUMMARY

✦ MBE ventures are seldom safe, easy, or comfortable. But they are honest, raw and truly reach people who need to be helped. Edginess is the wave of the future and the reality of now.

✦ True prosperity is available for anyone willing to commit himself to God and follow his ways.

✦ Visionaries don't listen to dream killers. They remind themselves of their calling and press onward. That is your invitation, today!

ENDNOTES

FOREWORD

1. See Matthew 6:33

INTRODUCTION

1. Andrew Murray, *Waiting On God,* Christian Literature Crusade: Fort Washington, PA, 1980 edition, p. 65

CHAPTER 1

1. http://www.barna.org/FlexPage.aspx?Page=BarnaUpdate&BarnaUpdate ID=187 accessed Feb 2009

2. Psalm 50:10 NIV

3. James 2:20

4. I Timothy 6:10

5. Matthew 21:2

6. Source: David Bornstein, *How to Change the World: Social Entrepreneurs and the Power of New Ideas,* Updated Edition, Oxford University Press, USA; Updated edition (September 17, 2007)

CHAPTER 2

1. Genesis 37:19 NIV

2. John 15:16 NIV

3. Genesis 39:8-10 NIV

4. See Matthew 25:40

5. Genesis 41:48-49

6. See Philippians 3:14

7. See Mark 12:30-31

8. See 2 Corinthians 9:7

9. See 1 Timothy 6:7

CHAPTER 3

1. See Hosea 12:6

2. 1 Timothy 3:2-3 NIV

3. 1 Timothy 3:2-7 NIV

4. 1 Timothy 3:3 NIV

5. See Luke 18:22

6. Proverbs 11:10 NIV

7. Hebrews 13:2 NIV

8. "Her husband is respected at the city gate, where he takes his seat among the elders of the land" (Proverbs 31:23 NIV)

9. Jeremiah 30:21 NIV

10. Galatians 2:20 NIV

11. George G. Hunter III, *The Celtic Way of Evangelism* (Nashville: Abingdon, 2000), p. 52

12. Ibid., p. 53

13. Ibid., p. 54

14. Genesis 37:19-20 NIV

15. Proverbs 29:18 KJV

16. Ephesians 3:20

17. Barbara Hudson, *The Henrietta Mears Story* (Grand Rapids, MI: Revell. 1957), p. 101

CHAPTER 4

1. *Today in the Word,* http://www.sermonillustrations.com/a-z/p/persever ance.htm accessed April 2009

CHAPTER 5

1. *Daily Bread,* June 6, 1986, quoted in: http://www.sermonillustrations. com/a-z/p/perseverance.htm accessed April 2009

2. John 1:14 *The Message*

3. 1 John 2:15 NIV

4. John 11: 25-26; 43-44 NIV

5. Habakkuk 2:2 KJV

CHAPTER 6

1. John 4:13-14 NIV

2. 1 Thessalonians 5:11 NIV

3. See John 13:34

CHAPTER 7

1. Adapted from Larry Cunningham (Billings, Montana), *Reader's Digest.* http://www.sermonillustrations.com/a-z/m/marriage.htm accessed April 2009

2. See Ephesians 4:26

3. Ephesians 5:25 NIV

4. See Philippians 2:7 KJV

5. Franklin, op. cit.

6. 1 Corinthians 13:5 NIV

7. M. Scott Peck, M.D., *The Road Less Traveled* (New York: Simon and Schuster, 2002 [25th Anniversary Edition]), p. 16

8. Charles Bracelen Flood, *Lee: the Last Years* (Mariner Books, 1998), quot ed in: Michael Williams, http://www.sermonillustrations.com/a-z/f/for giveness.htm accessed April 2009

CHAPTER 8

1. James 2:20 NKJV

2. Matthew 25:35

3. Proverbs 18:21 NIV

CHAPTER 9

1. Isaiah 58:10

2. Acts 2:42-47 NIV

CHAPTER 10

1. See Romans 12:2

2. See Ephesians 4:12

CHAPTER 11

1. Hosea 1:2 NLT

2. See Revelation 21:2

3. Hosea 2:7 NLT

4. Deuteronomy 28:13 NLT

5. Hosea 1:10-11 NLT (Emphasis added)

6. See Hosea 9:14-17

7. See Hosea 2:14-16

8. Hosea 3:1 NLT

9. Hosea 4:11 NLT

10. Hosea 4:16 NLT

11. See Revelation 2:4

12. Hosea 6:3 NLT

JOIN THE MBE REVOLUTION!

In this Appendix, you will learn more about how to join the "MBE Revolution" of mission-based entrepreneurs who launch faith-based businesses and social service ministries that Eric Bahme describes in his book. In addition to the Portland, OR, hotel properties described in his book, Pastor Eric and his associates have years of successful experience managing hotels for profit. They are available to share their expertise with others. The author assists MBEs, churches and ministries to develop their own hotel properties and launch social service ministries such as the My Father's House homeless shelter and the Freedom House recovery ministry in their cities.

HOW TO GET STARTED

Here are several ways you can join the MBE Revolution:

◆ Website. Getting started is as easy as finding the author's website, www.KingdomPoint.com and clicking on the links.

◆ Inquiry form. On the website, fill out the inquiry form and someone will contact you.

◆ Email. You can email the author at Eric@KingdomPoint.com.

◆ Introductory seminars. You can attend a Portland seminar or schedule your own to gain information to move forward.

◆ Speaking. You can invite Eric to speak at your church service or event and hear more transformational stories.

CHRISTIAN ASSET NETWORK (CAN)

Contact:	Eric Bahme
Address:	9727 NE Sandy Blvd
	Portland, OR 97220
Phone:	800-820-9759
Fax:	503-296-2459
Email:	eric@KingdomPoint.com
Web:	www.KingdomPoint.com

BACKGROUND

Throughout the book you have been introduced to some of the capabilities of the Christian Asset Network. Below are additional details on some of the services that are available to you.

OVERVIEW AND PURPOSE

CAN makes it possible for a ministry to purchase and operate a hotel that focuses on community transformation and sustainability of the investment. It's not about making money for its own sake. Rather, it's about using revenue to fund projects that transform communities. It's about people who refuse to sit idly by and watch a world in turmoil. Instead, they shout, "We will stand up! We will not rest! We will become the best."

BRIDGING THE GAP BETWEEN MINISTRY AND HOTELS

Operating a hotel is not a quick fix for ministry funding, but it is an achievable dream because of the number of resources available through CAN to help you become successful. CAN stands in the gap for those who have a desire to enter the hotel business and create a self-funding model for ministry. CAN is a bridge between two worlds—the world of ministry and the world of hotels. When you bring them together, you can create an impact on society within the framework of the Kingdom of God. You make a major difference in the lives of people. CAN helps you navigate the waters and answer questions like these:

◆ How should we structure our organization—profit or non-profit, or some of both?

◆ Where can we find a hotel property to purchase? How do we get funding?

◆ How do we operate a hotel on a day-to-day basis?

◆ How does a Christian hotel operate differently?

◆ How do we manage our record keeping?

◆ What should we do about marketing our hotel?

◆ How can we become more successful than our powerful competitors?

◆ How do we connect with our customers? What should we say and not say?

◆ How can we use the hotel to share Christ with our guests?

◆ What should we do about strategic planning and setting long term goals?

◆ Should we brand our hotel with a national flag?

◆ How can we make the most of our partnership with a valuable hotel brand?

◆ How do we hire and motivate excellent employees?

◆ When will we start making a profit?

◆ How can we use our conference center as a meeting place for the church?

◆ Should we establish a Freedom House on our campus?

◆ Should we build a local homeless shelter like My Father's House?

◆ How can our ministry be more involved in our city and develop our hotel as a positive community asset?

◆ Are there other ways we can be socially involved?

As you seek to answer these and other questions, we will be there to strengthen and teach you. The more you learn, the more you will in turn be able to teach others.

EVALUATION OF POTENTIAL HOTEL PROPERTIES

When you locate a hotel property that you might like to acquire, CAN has the resources to analyze the past and present financial performance of the lodging property or development. We can identify areas of potential liability and help you reduce your risks. We can analyze the terms in existing and proposed contracts. We can evaluate the performance of the current property management company and determine the effectiveness of the hotel's affiliation with a major chain. When there is a change of management, we work with legal counsel to negotiate the business terms of a new agreement and oversee the transition of management responsibilities. More importantly we can show you how to put grace and the message of the Gospel in the property you will run.

Strategic Alliances:

Over the years, we have built strategic alliances with individuals and companies who will be able to help the ministry prosper. You will not be locating resource people all by yourself. You enter a new world but you do not enter it alone. Although the worlds of business and ministry are different, it is possible to function in both worlds when you have an interpreter. Churches and hotel businesses may not speak the same language, but we have blended the two for the greater good of a new hospitality ministry.

BOTTOM LINE PROFIT AND GUEST SATISFACTION

In the hotel industry, your goal is to increase "revenue per available room" (REVPAR), which is a key industry measure of financial success. When your business operation is profitable, you have more money for ministry. CAN helps boost a hotel's performance by maintaining a distinctive hospitality experience while lowering costs. However, with us the bottom line is not only profit. It is guest satisfaction. It is attracting people to the experience we provide.

Hospitality refers to the relationship between guest and host. It follows the biblical model of entertaining strangers with a liberality of good will. When you treat people as if they are Christ, you open the door for them to share their lives with you. When you show them that your heart is sensitive to their needs, they want to return and when they return, your investment returns a profit.

CENTRALIZED NETWORK OF RESOURCES

CAN provides your business with a centralized network of resources. We have hands-on experience in the areas of finance, operations and marketing, including extensive market knowledge developed over a period of years. We bring to the table a central, independent, objective point of review and communication. As you develop your ministry's network of projects and resource people, we can help you align your interests with those of other participants.

Here are some of the services we provide for ongoing operations:

◆ Prepare strategic plan and annual business plan in harmony with Christian hospitality principles.

◆ Analyze financial performance data and conduct investor reporting on a periodic basis to maximize profits.

◆ Monitor competitive market and sales and marketing program performance on a periodic basis.

◆ Monitor loan performance and compliance.

◆ Analyze financial performance of the lodging properties or developments.

◆ Monitor compliance with existing management and brand-licensing agreements.

◆ Evaluate the performance of the management company.

◆ Select and supervise consultants and other professionals as appropriate.

◆ Negotiate, administer and monitor major contracts.

◆ Monitor key human resource issues and trends.

◆ Administer real estate tax and insurance programs.

◆ Help to negotiate through property tax issues and nonprofit status.

◆ Monitor physical condition of the asset.

◆ Approve/monitor annual capital expenditures.

◆ Develop a long-term capital expenditure plan.

◆ Monitor investment climate, sales prices and capitalization rates of comparable proprieties on a periodic basis.

◆ Monitor sales disposition and/or hotel refinancing alternatives on a periodic basis.

TURNKEY OPERATIONS FROM ESTABLISHED HOTEL CHAINS

Before you open for business, you will already have a team of people on board that we have brought alongside to help. You will be able to operate your hotel with skills that are the envy of the hotel trade. Your business will stand out as a place of impeccable order and profound peace. You will have documentation of policies and will be able to provide uniformly excellent service to your guests.

How does this work? Although many Christians think that they need to form their own models from scratch, we have found much greater success in working with the best models that already exist. Instead of encouraging you to stay behind church walls with a fortress mentality, we show you the benefits of moving into the business sector in an industry that is already established and where you can become a significant player.

The Portland Airport Convention Center that we own is branded under Choice Hotels. When I go to a Choice Hotels event, I rub shoulders with other people who do not necessarily share my Christian values, but I value them. I can be a witness to people "in the world" instead of retreating from the world.

I have found Choice Hotels people to be warm and considerate and they have made significant concessions to allow me to operate according to values that are important to us as a ministry. They have seen how our collaboration has increased their bottom line, which has given our ministry credibility and allowed us to prosper together.

CAN brings together people doing business in the secular world with ministries that operate by Christian values. This helps the Church to build and perform its mission. We don't have to create something new that is already being done well. We can take what already exists and modify it to match our values as Christians.

What makes our hospitality center mission-based is when Jesus moves in. We don't have to create a new concept for the practical details. We can take something that already exists and package it in our own unique style. That streamlines the process. We can provide the pieces when someone calls and says I want to start a hotel because we have already discovered the most reliable resource people and systems.

HOTEL MANAGEMENT COMPANIES THAT HELP YOU EVERY DAY

As a ministry that owns a hotel, you don't have to manage the daily operations yourself if you obtain the services of a high performance management company. They help you to succeed by providing services like in-depth management systems, human resource services and employee training. They are there to serve you. We know of outstanding Christians in secular management companies that can help you create an environment of shared goals and unified purpose while they are also helping you to succeed financially. They will share your concern for developing your employees as individuals at the same time as they show you how to serve your guests with kindness and excellent service.

DECISION MAKING ON DISTRESSED PROPERTIES

My wife said to me once, "Wherever we go, we always remodel!" Hotels like the one we purchased in Portland are called "distressed properties." If they are not turned around, they will fail. However, if the renovation process is successful, they will create value for the owner and investors.

If you find an older hotel property that you would like to renovate, you know from reading this book that we have experience in that field! Whether you want to tear down old buildings and rebuild or renovate an existing structure, as we did, we can help either way.

Here are some of the decisions involved where we can help provide guidance.

◆ Decide if this is a reasonable opportunity.

◆ Examine whether this company is saved or if it will probably fail regardless of what you do.

◆ Decide if your time and energy is well spent for remodeling or if the cost will be prohibitive.

◆ Analyze whether or not you will be able to remain open for business during renovations and how that will affect cash flow.

◆ Define short-term steps to encourage those involved, reverse negative cash flow and start restoring your business to health.

◆ Develop a plan of action that will lead to the creation and realization of value.

◆ Find the best financial model. If necessary, take steps to attract additional financing.

◆ Choose the hotel chain that you will join.

◆ Create a turnaround environment among your staff.

◆ Renovate the physical plant by a team effort led by good team leaders.

◆ Establish a plan for crisis management.

◆ Address long-term issues such as new products and services that you can provide in the future.

◆ Establish a strong management team in the areas of operations and management that will lead your company into future growth and profitability.

WINNING THE SUPPORT OF THE COMMUNITY

When you open a new hotel or rebuild an older one you often win community support. In many cities, when you renovate a distressed property that has become an eyesore or even a source of crime, as with our experience, you become an asset to the city. Where city officials may have been neutral toward you as a church entity in the past—or even hostile—they will now see you as an asset.

Taxes are one of the major issues that come between municipal governments and churches, straining relationships. The tax-free, non-profit status that churches enjoy makes them a drain on city funds. Business-minded civic leaders see churches as non-contributing entities while pastors view authorities as annoying sticklers for the rules.

However, the tax revenues and other bonuses that hotels bring to the city place municipal governments squarely behind them. A church within the city limits is both a church and a community leader. Lives will be changed and before long the city will find it cannot live without the church.

BIBLICAL ENTREPRENEURSHIP TRAINING

NEHEMIAH PROJECT INTERNATIONAL MINISTRIES

BACKGROUND

Patrice Tsague founded Nehemiah Project International Ministries (NPIM) in 1999 to help churches and individuals fulfill God's plan through business. Nehemiah's Biblical Entrepreneurship (BE) Training in churches and other locations in the U.S. and overseas trains Christians how to operate businesses that not only fund missions through company profits but also make the business itself a mission.

NPIM offers a proprietary certificate business course called "Biblical Entrepreneurship" that combines core business concepts and biblical principles. Courses include Principles of Biblical Entrepreneurship (BE I), Practices of Biblical Entrepreneurship (BE II) and Planning a Biblically-Based Business (BE III). Most graduates of the program have been able to start and operate small to medium sized businesses in the United States and other nations. The largest business to enroll and complete the course, generate over $12 million dollars in annual revenue. To date, NPIM has trained more than 1,300 students in the United States, Mexico, Ukraine, Europe and Cameroon. NPIM also offers alumni support services to its graduates.

In partnership with Eric Bahme, author of *The MBE Revolution* NPIM promotes a vision for Kingdom businesses backed by churches as a community transformation model.

Contact:	Patrice Tsague
Address:	Nehemiah Project International Ministries 24218 Arena Stage Court Damascus, MD 20872
Phone:	877-916-1180
Email:	info@nehemiahproject.org
Web:	www.nehemiahproject.org

When Eric Bahme's church, Eastside Foursquare Church of Portland, Oregon, hosted Nehemiah BE Training in October 2008, it became an opportunity not only to train hotel staff and those connected to the church but also to further expand the church's outreach into the community. People came to learn how to start and operate businesses successfully and as a result saw how they could sharpen and use the gifts that God has given them. They gained a sense of purpose in getting businesses started. After the seminar was over and Nehemiah had left town, the church's rapport with the entrepreneurial community expanded into other areas.

Once you have brought people into your church and taught them biblical entrepreneurship, a church that understands the business/ministry model can give potential business owners the push they need to get going. It can provide mentoring and nurturing. The church can be there for them when they need understanding and support. When they hit a few obstacles, someone from the church with more experience can come alongside and help them out. That makes the businessmen more likely to succeed and also keeps the church involved in individual and community transformation.

BE SEMINAR ADVANTAGES

◆ Pastors and business leaders start to see themselves as a team.

◆ Potential entrepreneurs realize that they can start businesses based on the Bible.

◆ Current business owners gain an understanding of succeeding in business biblically.

◆ Church leaders learn practical guidelines for supporting business owners and others in the marketplace.

◆ Churches gain a vision for community transformation if the church could own a business.

OPPORTUNITY FOR INTERNATIONAL INFLUENCE

One church with a business mindset can affect a whole city. It can also change a nation. In November 1998, Patrice's mother visited the United States and invited Patrice and his wife Gina to visit Cameroon, where he had been born. After they arrived in the country, they saw the desperate condition of many of the people. They taught a series of Bible studies, held prayer sessions, donated more than 70 French Bibles and led many people to Christ. While they were there, the Lord gave them a vision from the book of Nehemiah that eventually became reflected in their name. It was the beginning of their international outreach. To date more than 600 people in Cameroon have received Nehemiah BE training and several hundred are in business today.

Recently when a church in Mexico City wanted to uplift its community both economically and spiritually, they invited Nehemiah to train and certify 24 teachers who could teach BE seminars in other communities around the country. The church has a goal of teaching 3,000 people in the next year. If most of those 3,000 start successful businesses, it would have a tremendous impact on the Mexican economy. When churches understand the potential for community transformation through biblical entrepreneurship, the results will be unlimited and the Great Commission can be advanced into all the world.

FREEDOM HOUSE MINISTRIES

BACKGROUND

Freedom House is a faith-based residential recovery program on the campus of the hotels owned by Eastside Foursquare Church in Portland, Oregon, as described in the book *The MBE Revolution* by Eric Bahme. Freedom House recovery programs can also be established in your ministry or community.

Contact:	Pastor Jim Cottrell
Address:	Freedom House Ministries
	P.O. Box 33150
	Portland, OR 97292-3150
Phone:	503-347-9966
Email:	info@freedomhouseministries.net
Web:	www.freedomhouseministries.net

Freedom House successfully assists people desiring to find freedom from addictions and life-controlling problems. Its focus on developing consistent Christian character and a strong work ethic results in restored relationships. Graduates become productive citizens who contribute to their community. While providing discipleship training and character development, Freedom House offers recovery program opportunities based on biblical principles in a highly structured and accountable environment to enable students to become spiritually, physically and emotionally sound.

THE PROGRAM

Those attending Freedom House Ministries learn the cause of their addictions from a Christian perspective. At Freedom House, students are encouraged to turn to God as their hope for change.

Individuals are given the opportunity to establish and improve their relationship with God through private study and prayer, daily devotions, chapel services and biblical counseling. During their year of training students also have opportunities to apply biblical principles in work ethics and daily routines.

THREE LEVELS OF RECOVERY

The Freedom House program consists of three levels. Each level focuses on a restoration process for the individual. Residents are required to participate in regularly scheduled Bible instruction, individual counseling, work-study education and other life-changing activities.

Level One (12 Weeks)

The student receives guidance and structure that promotes a restored lifestyle. During this time individuals attend classes, receive biblical instruction and participate in assigned tasks and work projects.

Level Two (18 Weeks)

The student completes a series of classes to promote a personal relationship with Christ and to facilitate Christian maturity. Each student continues to participate in daily routines, expectations and work projects as he pursues an individual plan focused on his specific personal problems and family issues.

Level Three (22 Weeks)

The student is a given increased independence within the established expectation of accountability and responsibility. Individuals become more involved as role-models and mentors to others in the program. During this transition period, students are assigned increased responsibility along with individual studies and biblical instruction.

MY FATHER'S HOUSE COMMUNITY SHELTERS

BACKGROUND

Dan and Cathe Wiese opened their first shelter for the homeless in a duplex that housed five families but soon had to turn away an average of 112 families every month. With community support and private grants they built a new My Father's House shelter, a three-story, 27,000 square foot, $3.9 million building project with 30 individual apartments. It is the largest facility of its kind without government support in the United States.

Contact:	Dan and Cathe Wiese
Address:	My Father's House
	PO Box 1147
	Gresham, OR 97030
Phone:	503-492-3046
Email:	cathe@familyshelter.org
Web:	www.mfhshelter.org

THE PROGRAM

The average age of a homeless person in the Portland area is nine years old, with more homeless families than singles. Each unit provides a safe place where a family can start a new life. It has an outside lock with a key entry like a hotel, individual heat and air conditioning, a private bathroom with new linens for each family, a kitchenette with refrigerator and microwave. My Father's House includes job counseling and teaches parenting skills. An on-site chapel and daily programs restore people to a normal life. My Father's House has an incredible 85 percent success rate.

AUTHOR ERIC BAHME

(PRONOUNCED "BAME")

As a cutting edge entrepreneur, Eric is the founder and president of NEO International Christian ministries; a national non-profit organization created to network and empower other ministries. He also serves as the founding Pastor of Eastside Foursquare Church (http://www.eastsidechurch.net), a congregation that has grown significantly in the last five years on a large hotel campus that the church owns. Eric sits on several for profit and non-profit boards including Genesis Hotel Partners, Lincoln Asset Management and My Father's House, the only year round family shelter in Gresham, Oregon.

Contact:	Eric Bahme
Address:	9727 NE Sandy Blvd
	Portland, OR 97220
Phone:	800-820-9759
Fax:	503-296-2459
Email:	eric@KingdomPoint.com
Web:	www.KingdomPoint.com

Born in Arizona, Eric knew from an early age that he wanted to enter the ministry in spite of being raised in a non-Christian home. He began preparing himself for the ministry, attending Walla Walla College and earning bachelor's degrees in theology and communication. Upon graduation, he and his wife Rita moved to Michigan, where Eric completed his Master's of Divinity. Moving to Seattle, they accepted their first job as senior pastors of New Life Christian Fellowship, where they served for 13 years.

In 2002, Eric and Rita moved with their daughter Alyssa to Portland, Oregon and founded Eastside Foursquare Church, giving birth to a new entrepreneurial model of ministry. During this time, Eric also became a managing partner in Lincoln Asset Management, one of the top 100 hospitality management companies in the United

States, successfully initiating and expanding the company's management contract business and ownership. In addition, Eric is a partner in Genesis Hotels LLC, a network of franchised hotels throughout the Northwest.

Through the Christian Asset Network (CAN), Eric and his partners provide a network of hotel developers to pastors and other mission-based entrepreneurs who aspire to acquire income-producing hotel businesses to help fund their outreach ministries. An inspiring and energizing speaker, Eric helps organizations harness the unique power of their business and ministry communities to achieve extraordinary leaps in performance. He is a visionary storyteller with a gift for teaching organizations how to inspire passion in their people and tap their collective intelligence. His fast-moving talks are full of valuable insights and practical applications.